C0-FVP-392

MICHIGAN
CHRISTIAN
COLLEGE
LIBRARY
ROCHESTER, MICH.

226.1
B582j

314
32

BT
299.2
.J4
1982

AN AMERICAN CHRISTIAN BIBLE

Extracted by

THOMAS JEFFERSON

Together with
A New Declaration of Independence
for Today's Americans, by Erik Holden

Published by
SOVEREIGN PRESS
326 Harris Road
Rochester, WA 98579

MICHIGAN
CHRISTIAN
COLLEGE
LIBRARY
ROCHESTER, MICH.

Copyright © Erik Holden 1982

All rights reserved — no part of this book
may be reproduced in any form without permission
in writing from the copyright owner.

ISBN 0-914752-14-6

Library of Congress Catalog Card Number 82-80548

Manufactured in the United States of America

INTRODUCTION

The relationship between religion and government will be a continuing concern in this presentation of Thomas Jefferson's extracts from the Gospels.

The Declaration of Independence is the world's best known and most emphatic statement that there should be no government except by agreement between those being governed. This is declared to be self-evident — yet it is stated.

Stating it had become necessary because dogma that contradicted the self-evident had been imposed on the Northern European ancestors of the American colonists for over a thousand years.

Dogma is a system, or conglomerate, of ideas and statements that are presented as "authoritative." Acceptance of dogma is initially imposed by force. When forced acceptance has long continued, all cease to question. Then it becomes necessary to restate the self-evident. People, Jefferson said, "are more disposed to suffer while evils are sufferable than to right themselves by abolishing the forms to which they are accustomed."

Thomas Jefferson, author of the Declaration of Independence, knew that dogma is the primary weapon of the unscrupulous. All around him he saw the continuation of the dogma that had been imposed on the Northern Europeans by inquisitions that were called "Christian." At the same time it was evident to Jefferson that Jesus had been crucified because of his opposition to dogma.

Jefferson separated himself from the established churches of his day. Discarding both the Old Testament Bible of the Jews, and the works of Paul, he cut from the gospels of

32416

Matthew, Mark, Luke and John, the basic story and teachings of Jesus. In a letter to John Adams, dated October 12, 1813, he said these were "as easily distinguished as diamonds in a dung-hill."

The book Jefferson made by pasting the cut out portions into a continuous form he titled "The Life and Morals of Jesus of Nazareth, Extracted texturally from the Gospels." Recognizing the need to keep his work secret, he succeeded in doing so. It was not made public until 1902. At that time, the newly discovered work was called "The Jefferson Bible." It has here been designated, "An American Christian Bible." In 1904, the Government Printing Office, as directed by resolution of the Fifty-seventh Congress, printed 9,000 copies — 3,000 for use of the Senate and 6,000 for the use of the House. The original — height 8¼ inches, width 4-13/16 inches, thickness in middle 1¼ inches — is now in The National Museum of American History.

As a scholar, Jefferson was interested in the parallel between the execution of Socrates and the execution of Jesus. He was also concerned with determining what version of the Bible was probably the most accurate. His work, and the copies printed for Congress, contained, side by side, the same text cut from Greek, Latin, French and English Bibles. A photographic copy of the English portion is reprinted here.

Standing alone, the arrangement made by Jefferson gives no new general significance to the various texts elsewhere available. With his aversion to dogma, he certainly would not have wanted his arrangement to be presented with the implication that it came from a famous man and should therefore be accepted as "authoritative."

At present, however it does have a specific significance for the American people because pressure to accept ideas presented as "authoritative" is becoming an intense issue. The media and the schools are both involved. The increasing control of the media by those opposing the principles on which the United States was founded is a problem of major concern. Teaching "science" called "religion," and "religion" called "science," in tax supported schools is causing conflict between opposing groups.

Careful interpretation of the First Amendment to the United States Constitution is of vital importance. The *intent* of those originally writing the law is a heavily weighted factor when a law is being interpreted. The Declaration of Independence is the basic document setting forth the *intent* underlying the *very existence of the United States.* It contains the pertinent words "Nature and Nature's God." A determination of what those words meant to the writer is significant. The extracts from the Bible made by Jefferson are pertinent to that determination.

That alone is adequate reason for again bringing this work to public attention. But I want to place it in a wider context. The controversy over the First Amendment readily falls into a context wide enough to include not only all the people of the present world but the history and destiny of the entire human species.

A distorted presentation of human knowledge, and the use of unperceptive, dogma-controlled groups to breed out perceptive individuals, has long overruled natural selection. Failure to accept the way of nature and nature's god points toward a biological human destiny far worse than that threatened by atomic war. Jefferson, and Jefferson's view of Jesus, make a good starting point for consideration of significant aspects that have received too little attention.

A solid basis existed for Jefferson's approval of Jesus that would have puzzled people of his day. His extracts from the gospels cut away every implication that Jesus was a "supernatural" being. In a letter January 9, 1816, Jefferson wrote to Charles Thomson, "*I* am a *real Christian*." Jefferson could see that both he and Jesus were fighting dogma. Jesus had been crucified by reason of that fight. Many of Jefferson's friends had died in the fight against dogma used as a basis for British tyranny. In preparation for that fight, Jefferson had written that "we mutually pledge to each other, our lives, our Fortunes, and our sacred Honor," and he had been as ready to die as had been Jesus and Jefferson's friends. The fight against dogma is long and bloody.

Dogma has been with us since long before recorded history. It distorts our perception. It sticks to us like a tarry substance. The methods we must use for removing it often damage vital tissue. And still much of the sticky stuff from the past remains. Sincere scholars, as well as dogma-makers looking for a way to destroy the efforts of the perceptive, can find some of the sticky stuff on both the "historical Jefferson" and the "historical Jesus." However, if history is not to be "a tale told by an idiot," it must focus on what is vital. This means ignoring both the retained tar and whatever mutilation of living tissue was done in the process of trying to remove it. It means focusing exclusively on the path of the vital continuity.

In paring down the teachings of Jesus, Jefferson may have cut into a part that has become vital in our day. Dogma-makers attack any area where defenses have been lowered. Popular Materialism, called "science" by the pseudo-science's high priests, has a new dogma that Jefferson did not have to confront.

The present pseudo-scientist's purportedly "authoritative" pronouncement that creative intelligence can evolve from something other than creative intelligence has become a new dogma. It may be even more destructive of perception than the "supernatural" one forced on the Northern Europeans in the name of "Christianity." Present conditions require that this new dogma be viewed as a continuation of the same non-natural direction.

I want to continue the fight against dogma as waged by Jesus and Jefferson. In my fight, I have chosen to begin with the story of Jesus from which all dogma of the "supernatural" was cut away by Jefferson.

Jesus pointed out the only two possible directions for human destiny. I have tried to put these into a perspective that includes current developments. Readers who already think of the life, teachings, and crucifixion of Jesus without the surrounding "supernatural" dogma may find it unnecessary to review the purged extracts before looking at a view of these *only* two possible directions in the context of current knowledge.

Erik Holden

The

LIFE AND MORALS

of

JESUS OF NAZARETH

Extracted textually from the Gospels

by

THOMAS JEFFERSON

A Table

of the Texts ~~of this Extract~~ from the Evangelists employed in this Narrative, and of the order of their arrangement.

page	
1.	Luke.2.1–7. Joseph & Mary go to Bethlehem, where Jesus is born.
	21.39. he is circumcised & named. & they return to Nazareth.
	40.42–48.51.52. at 12. years of age he accompanies his
2.	parents to Jerusalem and returns.
	L.3.1.2. Mk.1.4 Mt.3.4.5.6. John baptises in Jordan.
	Mt.3.13. Jesus is baptised. L.3.23. at 30. years of age.
3.	J.2.12–16. drives the traders out of the temple.
	J.3.22. Mt.4.12. Mk.6.17–28. he ~~goes~~ baptises but retires into Galilee on the death of Jn.
4.	[illegible] Mk.1.21.22. he teaches in the Synagogue.
5.	Mt.12.1–5.9–12. Mk.2.27. Mt.12.14.15. explains the Sabbath.
	L.6.12–17. call of his disciples.
6.	Mt.5.1–12. L.6.24.25.26. Mt.5.13–47. L.6.34.35.36. Mt.6.1–34.7.1.
to 15.	L.6.30. Mt.7.3–20.12.35.36.37 7.24–29. the Sermon in the Mount.
	Mt.8.1. Mk.6.6. Mt.11.28.29.30. exhorts.
16.	L.7.36–46. a woman anointeth him.
17.	Mk.3.31–35. L.12.1–7. 13–15 precepts
18.	L.12.16–21. parable of the rich man.
.20	22–48.54.59. L.13.1–5 precepts.
21.	L.13.6–9. parable of the figtree.
22.	L.11.37–46.52.53.54. precepts.
23.	Mt.13.1–9. Mk.4.10. Mt.13.18–23. parable of the Sower.
4.25	Mk.4.21.22.23. precepts. Mt.13.24–30.36–52. parable of the Tares.
.27	Mk.4.26–34. L.9.57–62. L.5.27–29. Mk.2.15–17 precepts
	L.5.36–39. parable of new wine in old bottles.
28.	Mt.13.53–57. a prophet hath no honor in his own country.
29.	Mt.9.36. Mk.6.7. Mt.10.5.6.9–18.23.26–31. Mk.6.12.30. mission, instrn, return of apostles
30.31.	J.7.1. Mk.7.1–5.14–24. Mt.18.1–4.7–9.12–17.21–~~22~~35. precepts.
33.	Mt.18.23.–35. parable of the wicked servant.

page	
34.	L. 10. 1—8. 10—12. mission of the LXX.
35	J. 7. 2—16. 19—26. 32. 43—53. the feast of the tabernacles.
36.	J. 8. 1—11. the woman taken in Adultery.
37.	J. 9. 1. 2. 3. to be born blind no proof of sin.
	J. 10. 1—5. 11.—14. 16. the good shepherd.
38.	L. 10. 25—37. love god & thy neighbor. parable of the Samaritan.
39.	L. 11. 1—13. form of prayer.
40.	L. 14. 1—6. the Sabbath.
41.	7—24. the bidden to a feast.
42.	28—32. precepts.
43.44	L. 15. 1—32. parables of the lost sheep and Prodigal son.
45.	L. 16. 1—15. parable of the unjust steward.
46.	18—31. parable of Lazarus.
47.48.	L. 17. 1—4. 7—10. 20. 26—36. precepts to be always ready.
49.	L. 18. 1—14. parables of the widow & judge, the Pharisee & Publican.
50.51.	L. 10. 38—42. Mt. 19. 1—26. precepts.
52.	Mt. 20. 1—16. parable of the laborers in the vineyard.
53.54.	L. 19. 1—28. Zaccheus, & the parable of the talents.
55.56.	Mt. 21. 1—3. 6—8. 10. J. 12. 19—24. Mt. 21. 17. goes to Jerusalem & Bethany.
	Mk. 11. 12. 15—19. the traders cast out from the temple.
	Mk. 11. 27. Mt. 21. 27—31. parable of the two sons.
57.	Mt. 21. 33. Mk. 12. 1—9. Mt. 21. 45. 46. parable of the vineyard & husbandmen.
58.	Mt. 22. 1.—14. parable of the king and wedding.
59.	15—33. tribute. marriage. resurrection.
60.	Mk. 12. 28—31. Mt. 22. 40. Mk. 12. 32. 33. the two commandments.
61.62	Mt. 23. 1—33. precepts. pride. hypocrisy. swearing.
63.	Mk. 12. 41—44. the widow's mite.
64.	Mt. 24. 1. 2. 16—21. 32. 33. 36—39. 40—44. Jerusalem & the day of judgment.
	45—51. the faithful and wise servant.
65.	Mt. 25. 1—13. parable of the ten virgins.
66.	14—30. parable of the talents.
67.68	L. 21. 34—36. Mt. 25. 31—46. the day of judgment.
69.	Mk. 14. 1—8. a woman anointeth him.

Mt. 26. 14–16. Judas undertakes to point out Jesus.

70. 71. 17–20. L. 22. 24–27. J. 13. 2. 4–17. 21–26. 31. 34. 35. Mt. 26. 31. 33.

72. L. 22. 33–34. Mt. 26. 35–45. precepts to his disciples, washes their feet, trouble of mind and prayer.

73. J. 18. 1–3. Mt. 26. 48–50. Judas conducts the officers to Jesus.

74. J. 18. 4–8. Mt. 26. 50–52. 55. 56. Mk. 14. 51. 52. Mt. 26. 57. J. 18. 15. 16. 18. 17.

75. J. 18. 25. 26. 27. Mt. 26. 75. J. 18. 19–23. Mk. 14. 55–61.
L. 22. 67. 68. 70. Mk. 14. 63–65. he is arrested & carried before Caiaphas the High priest & is condemned.

76. J. 18. 28–31. 33–38. L. 23. 5. Mt. 27. 13. is then carried to Pilate.

77. L. 23. 6–12. who sends him to Herod.

78. L. 23. 13–16. Mt. 27. 15–23. 26. recieves him back, scourges and delivers him to execution.

79. 80. Mt. 27. 27. 29–31. 3–8. L. 23. 26–32. J. 19. 17–24. Mt. 27. 39–43.

81. L. 23. 39–41. 34. J. 19. 25–27. Mt. 27. 46–[illegible] 55. 56. his crucifixion, death and burial.

J. 19. 31–34. 38–42. Mt. 27. 60. his burial.

CHAP. II. L.

The Roman empire taxed.

AND it came to pass in those days, that there went out a decree from Cesar Augustus, that all the world should be taxed.

2 (*And* this taxing was first made when Cyrenius was governor of Syria.)

3 And all went to be taxed, every one into his own city.

4 And Joseph also went up from Galilee, out of the city of Nazareth, into Judea, unto the city of David, which is called Beth-lehem (because he was of the house and lineage of David,)

5 To be taxed with Mary his espoused wife, being great with child.

6 And so it was, that, while they were there, the days were accomplished that she should be delivered

7 And she brought forth her first-born son, and wrapped him in swaddling-clothes, and laid him in a manger; because there was no room for them in the inn.

21 And when eight days were accomplished for the circumcising of the child, his name was called JESUS,

39 And when they had performed all things according to the law of the Lord, they returned into Galilee, to their own city Nazareth.

40 And the child grew, and waxed strong in spirit, filled with wisdom;

42 And when he was twelve years old, they went up to Jerusalem, after the custom of the feast.

43 And when they had fulfilled the days, as they returned, the child Jesus tarried behind in Jerusalem; and Joseph and his mother knew not *of it*.

44 But they supposing him to have been in the company, went a day's journey; and they sought him among *their* kinsfolk and acquaintance.

45 And when they found him not, they turned back again to Jerusalem, seeking him.

46 And it came to pass, that after three days they found him in the temple, sitting in the midst of the doctors, both hearing them, and asking them questions. L.2.

47 And all that heard him were astonished at his understanding and answers.

48 And when they saw him, they were amazed: and his mother said unto him, Son, why hast thou thus dealt with us? behold, thy father and I have sought thee sorrowing.

51 And he went down with them, and came to Nazareth, and was subject unto them:

52 And Jesus increased in wisdom and stature,

NOW in the fifteenth year of the reign of Tiberius Cesar, Pontius Pilate being governor of Judea, and Herod being tetrarch of Galilee, and his brother Philip tetrarch of Iturea and of the region of Trachonitis, and Lysanias the tetrarch of Abilene, L.3

2 Annas and Caiaphas being the high priests,

4 John did baptize in the wilderness, M.1.

4 And the same John had his raiment of camels' hair, and a leathern girdle about his loins; and his meat was locusts and wild honey. M.3

5 Then went out to him Jerusalem, and all Judea, and all the region round about Jordan.

6 And were baptized of him in Jordan,

13 Then cometh Jesus from Galilee to Jordan unto John, to be baptized of him. M.3.

23 And Jesus himself began to be about thirty years of age, L.3.

12 After this he went down to Capernaum, he, and his mother, and his brethren, and his disciples; and they continued there not many days. J.2.

13 And the Jews' passover was at hand; and Jesus went up to Jerusalem, J.2.

14 And found in the temple those that sold oxen, and sheep, and doves, and the changers of money, sitting:

15 And, when he had made a scourge of small cords, he drove them all out of the temple, and the sheep, and the oxen; and poured out the changers' money, and overthrew the tables;

16 And said unto them that sold doves, Take these things hence; make not my Father's house an house of merchandise.

22 After these things came Jesus and his disciples into the land of Judea; and there he tarried with them, and baptized. J.3.

12 Now, when Jesus had heard that John was cast into prison, he departed into Galilee: Mt.4

17 For Herod himself had sent forth, and laid hold upon John, and bound him in prison for Herodias' sake, his brother Philip's wife: for he had married her. Mk.6

18 For John had said unto Herod, It is not lawful for thee to have thy brother's wife.

19 Therefore Herodias had a quarrel against him, and would have killed him; but she could not.

20 For Herod feared John, knowing that he was a just man, and an holy, and observed him; and when he heard him, he did many things, and heard him gladly.

21 And when a convenient day was come, that Herod, on his birth-day, made a supper to his lords, high captains, and chief *estates* of Galilee;

22 And when the daughter of the said Herodias came in and danced, and pleased Herod, and them that sat with him, the king said unto the damsel, Ask of me whatsoever thou wilt, and I will give *it* thee.

23 And he sware unto her, Whatsoever thou shalt ask of me, I will give *it* thee, unto the half of my kingdom.

24 And she went forth, and said unto her mother, What shall I ask? and she said, The head of John the Baptist. Mk.6.

25 And she came in straightway with haste unto the king, and asked, saying, I will that thou give me, by and by in a charger, the head of John the Baptist.

26 And the king was exceeding sorry; *yet* for his oath's sake, and for their sakes which sat with him, he would not reject her.

27 And immediately the king sent an executioner, and commanded his head to be brought: and he went and beheaded him in the prison;

28 And brought his head in a charger, and gave it to the damsel: and the damsel gave it to her mother.

21 And they went into Capernaum; and straightway on the sabbath-day, he entered into the synagogue, and taught. Mk.1.

22 And they were astonished at his doctrine: for he taught them as one that had authority, and not as the scribes.

AT that time Jesus went on the sabbath-day through the corn; and his disciples were an hungered, and began to pluck the ears of corn, and to eat. Mt.12.

2 But when the Pharisees saw *it*, they said unto him, Behold, thy disciples do that which is not lawful to do upon the sabbath-day.

3 But he said unto them, Have ye not read what David did when he was an hungered, and they that were with him;

4 How he entered into the house of God, and did eat the shewbread, which was not lawful for him to eat, neither for them which were with him, but only for the priests?

5 Or, have ye not read in the law, how that on the sabbath-days, the priests in the temple profane the sabbath, and are blameless?

9 And when he was departed M. 12
thence, he went into their syna-
gogue:
10 And, behold, there was a
man which had *his* hand wither-
ed. And they asked him, say-
ing, Is it lawful to heal on the
sabbath-days? that they might
accuse him.
11 And he said unto them,
What man shall there be among
you, that shall have one sheep,
and if it fall into a pit on the sab-
bath-day, will he not lay hold on
it, and lift *it* out?
12 How much then is a man
better than a sheep? Wherefore it
is lawful to do well on the sab-
bath-days.
27 And he said unto them, The Mk. 2
sabbath was made for man, and
not man for the sabbath:
14 Then the Pharisees went out, M. 12
and held a council against him,
how they might destroy him.
15 But when Jesus knew *it*, he
withdrew himself from thence:
and great multitudes followed
him,
12 And it came to pass in those L. 6.
days, that he went up into a
mountain to pray, and continued
all night in prayer to God.
13 And when it was day, he call-
ed *unto him* his disciples; and of
them he chose twelve, whom also
he named Apostles;
14 Simon, (whom he also named
Peter,) and Andrew his brother,
James and John, Philip and Bar-
tholomew,
15 Matthew and Thomas, James
the son of Alpheus, and Simon
called Zelotes,
16 And Judas *the brother* of
James, and Judas Iscariot, which
also was the traitor.
17 And he came down with
them, and stood in the plain; and
the company of his disciples, and
a great multitude of people out
of all Judea and Jerusalem, and
from the sea-coast of Tyre and
Sidon, which came to hear him,

AND seeing the multitudes, M. 5
he went up into a mountain:
and when he was set, his disci-
ples came unto him:
2 And he opened his mouth,
and taught them, saying,
3 Blessed *are* the poor in spirit:
for their's is the kingdom of hea-
ven.
4 Blessed *are* they that mourn:
for they shall be comforted.
5 Blessed *are* the meek: for
they shall inherit the earth.
6 Blessed *are* they which do
hunger and thirst after righteous-
ness: for they shall be filled.
7 Blessed *are* the merciful: for
they shall obtain mercy.
8 Blessed *are* the pure in heart:
for they shall see God.
9 Blessed *are* the peace-makers:
for they shall be called the chil-
dren of God.
10 Blessed *are* they which are
persecuted for righteousness'
sake: for their's is the kingdom
of heaven.
11 Blessed *are* ye when *men* shall
revile you, and persecute *you*,
and shall say all manner of evil
against you falsely, for my sake.
12 Rejoice, and be exceeding
glad; for great *is* your reward in
heaven: for so persecuted they the
prophets which were before you.
24 But woe unto you that are L.
rich! for ye have received your
consolation.
25 Woe unto you that are full!
for ye shall hunger. Woe unto
you that laugh now! for ye shall
mourn and weep.
26 Woe unto you when all men
shall speak well of you! for so did
their fathers to the false prophets.
13 Ye are the salt of the earth: M
but if the salt have lost his savour,
wherewith shall it be salted: it
is thenceforth good for nothing,
but to be cast out, and to be trod-
den under foot of men.
14 Ye are the light of the world.
A city that is set on an hill can-
not be hid.

M. 5.

15 Neither do men light a candle, and put it under a bushel, but on a candlestick, and it giveth light unto all that are in the house.

16 Let your light so shine before men, that they may see your good works, and glorify your Father which is in heaven.

17 Think not that I am come to destroy the law, or the prophets: I am not come to destroy, but to fulfil.

18 For verily I say unto you, Till heaven and earth pass, one jot or one tittle shall in no wise pass from the law, till all be fulfilled.

19 Whosoever, therefore, shall break one of these least commandments and shall teach men so, he shall be called the least in the kingdom of heaven: but whosoever shall do, and teach *them*, the same shall be called great in the kingdom of heaven.

20 For I say unto you, That except your righteousness shall exceed *the righteousness* of the scribes and Pharisees, ye shall in no case enter into the kingdom of heaven.

21 Ye have heard that it was said by them of old time, Thou shalt not kill; and, whosoever shall kill, shall be in danger of the judgment:

22 But I say unto you, That whosoever is angry with his brother without a cause, shall be in danger of the judgment: and whosoever shall say to his brother, Raca, shall be in danger of the council: but whosoever shall say, Thou fool, shall be in danger of hell fire.

23 Therefore, if thou bring thy gift to the altar, and there rememberest that thy brother hath aught against thee;

24 Leave there thy gift before the altar, and go thy way; first be reconciled to thy brother, and then come and offer thy gift.

M. 5.

25 Agree with thine adversary quickly, whilst thou art in the way with him; lest at any time the adversary deliver thee to the judge, and the judge deliver thee to the officer, and thou be cast into prison.

26 Verily I say unto thee, Thou shalt by no means come out thence, till thou hast paid the uttermost farthing.

27 Ye have heard that it was said by them of old time, Thou shalt not commit adultery:

28 But I say unto you, That whosoever looketh on a woman to lust after her, hath committed adultery with her already in his heart.

29 And if thy right eye offend thee, pluck it out, and cast it from thee: for it is profitable for thee, that one of thy members should perish, and not *that* thy whole body should be cast into hell.

30 And if thy right hand offend thee, cut it off, and cast *it* from thee: for it is profitable for thee, that one of thy members should perish, and not *that* thy whole body should be cast into hell.

31 It hath been said, Whosoever shall put away his wife, let him give her a writing of divorcement:

32 But I say unto you, That whosoever shall put away his wife, saving for the cause of fornication, causeth her to commit adultery: and whosoever shall marry her that is divorced, committeth adultery.

33 Again, ye have heard that it hath been said by them of old time, Thou shalt not forswear thyself, but shalt perform unto the Lord thine oaths:

34 But I say unto you, Swear not at all: neither by heaven; for it is God's throne:

35 Nor by the earth: for it is his

footstool: neither by Jerusalem; for it is the city of the great King: M. 5.

36 Neither shalt thou swear by thy head; because thou canst not make one hair white or black.

37 But let your communication be, Yea, yea; Nay, nay: for whatsoever *is* more than these cometh of evil.

38 Ye have heard that it hath been said, An eye for an eye, and a tooth for a tooth:

39 But I say unto you, That ye resist not evil: but whosoever shall smite thee on thy right cheek, turn to him the other also.

40 And if any man will sue thee at the law, and take away thy coat, let him have *thy* cloak also.

41 And whosoever shall compel thee to go a mile, go with him twain.

42 Give to him that asketh thee; and from him that would borrow of thee, turn not thou away.

43 Ye have heard that it hath been said, Thou shalt love thy neighbour, and hate thine enemy:

44 But I say unto you, Love your enemies, bless them that curse you, do good to them that hate you, and pray for them which despitefully use you, and persecute you;

45 That ye may be the children of your Father which is in heaven: for he maketh his sun to rise on the evil and on the good, and sendeth rain on the just and on the unjust.

46 For if ye love them which love you, what reward have ye? do not even the publicans the same?

47 And if ye salute your brethren only, what do ye more *than others?* do not even the publicans so?

34 And if ye lend *to them* of whom ye hope to receive, what thank have ye? for sinners also lend to sinners, to receive as much again. L. 6

35 But love ye your enemies, and do good, and lend, hoping for nothing again: and your reward shall be great, and ye shall be the children of the Highest: for he is kind unto the unthankful, and *to* the evil.

36 Be ye, therefore, merciful, as your Father also is merciful.

M. 6

TAKE heed that ye do not your alms before men, to be seen of them: otherwise ye have no reward of your Father which is in heaven.

2 Therefore, when thou doest *thine* alms, do not sound a trumpet before thee, as the hypocrites do in the synagogues, and in the streets, that they may have glory of men. Verily I say unto you, They have their reward.

3 But when thou doest alms, let not thy left hand know what thy right hand doeth:

4 That thine alms may be in secret: and thy Father, which seeth in secret, himself shall reward thee openly.

5 And when thou prayest, thou shalt not be as the hypocrites *are:* for they love to pray standing in the synagogues, and in the corners of the streets, that they may be seen of men. Verily I say unto you, They have their reward.

6 But thou, when thou prayest, enter into thy closet; and, when thou hast shut thy door, pray to thy Father which is in secret; and thy Father which seeth in secret, shall reward thee openly.

7 But when ye pray, use not vain repetitions, as the heathen *do:* for they think that they shall be heard for their much speaking.

8 Be not ye, therefore, like unto them: for your Father knoweth what things ye have need of, before ye ask him.

Mt. 6.

9 After this manner, therefore, pray ye: Our Father which art in heaven; Hallowed be thy name.

10 Thy kingdom come. Thy will be done in earth, as *it is* in heaven.

11 Give us this day our daily bread.

12 And forgive us our debts, as we forgive our debtors.

13 And lead us not into temptation; but deliver us from evil: For thine is the kingdom, and the power, and the glory, for ever. Amen.

14 For if ye forgive men their trespasses, your heavenly Father will also forgive you:

15 But if ye forgive not men their trespasses, neither will your Father forgive your trespasses.

16 Moreover, when ye fast, be not as the hypocrites, of a sad countenance: for they disfigure their faces, that they may appear unto men to fast. Verily I say unto you, They have their reward.

17 But thou, when thou fastest, anoint thine head, and wash thy face;

18 That thou appear not unto men to fast, but unto thy Father which is in secret: and thy Father, which seeth in secret, shall reward thee openly.

19 Lay not up for yourselves treasures upon earth, where moth and rust doth corrupt, and where thieves break through and steal:

20 But lay up for yourselves treasures in heaven, where neither moth nor rust doth corrupt, and where thieves do not break through nor steal:

21 For where your treasure is, there will your heart be also.

22 The light of the body is th eye: if, therefore, thine eye be single, thy whole body shall be full of light.

Mt. 6

23 But if thine eye be evil, thy whole body shall be full of darkness. If, therefore, the light that is in thee be darkness, how great *is* that darkness?

24 No man can serve two masters: for either he will hate the one, and love the other; or else he will hold to the one, and despise the other. Ye cannot serve God and mammon.

25 Therefore I say unto you, Take no thought for your life, what ye shall eat or what ye shall drink; nor yet for your body, what ye shall put on. Is not the ife more than meat, and the body than raiment?

26 Behold the fowls of the air: or they sow not, neither do they eap, nor gather into barns; yet our heavenly Father feedeth hem. Are ye not much better han they?

27 Which of you, by taking hought, can add one cubit unto his stature?

28 And why take ye thought for raiment? Consider the lilies of he field how they grow: they oil not, neither do they spin;

29 And yet I say unto you, That even Solomon in all his glory was not arrayed like one of these.

30 Wherefore, if God so clothe he grass of the field, which to day is, and to morrow is cast into the oven, *shall he* not much more *clothe* you? O ye of little faith;

31 Therefore, take no thought, saying, What shall we eat? or, What shall we drink? or, Wherewithal shall we be clothed?

32 (For after all these things do the Gentiles seek:) for your heavenly Father knoweth that ye have need of all these things.

33 But seek ye first the kingdom of God, and his righteousness; and all these things shall be added unto you.

34 Take therefore no thought for the morrow: for the morrow shall take thought for the things of itself. Sufficient unto the day *is* the evil thereof.

JUDGE not, that ye be not judged. M. 7

2 For with what judgment ye judge, ye shall be judged: and with what measure ye mete, it shall be measured to you again.

38 Give, and it shall be given unto you; good measure, pressed down, and shaken together, and running over, shall men give into your bosom. L. 6

3 And why beholdest thou the mote that is in thy brother's eye, but considerest not the beam that is in thine own eye? M. 7

4 Or how wilt thou say to thy brother, Let me pull out the mote out of thine eye; and, behold, a beam *is* in thine own eye?

5 Thou hypocrite! first cast out the beam out of thine own eye; and then shalt thou see clearly to cast out the mote out of thy brother's eye.

6 Give not that which is holy unto the dogs; neither cast ye your pearls before swine, lest they trample them under their feet, and turn again and rend you.

7 Ask, and it shall be given you; seek, and ye shall find; knock, and it shall be opened unto you:

8 For every one that asketh, receiveth; and he that seeketh, findeth; and to him that knocketh, it shall be opened.

9 Or what man is there of you, whom if his son ask bread, will he give him a stone?

10 Or if he ask a fish, will he give him a serpent?

11 If ye then, being evil, know how to give good gifts unto your children, how much more shall your Father, which is in heaven, give good things to them that ask him?

12 Therefore all things whatsoever ye would that men should do to you, do ye even so to them: for this is the law and the prophets.

13 Enter ye in at the strait gate; for wide *is* the gate, and broad *is* the way, that leadeth to destruction, and many there be which go in thereat: M. 7

14 Because strait *is* the gate, and narrow *is* the way, which leadeth unto life, and few there be that find it.

15 Beware of false prophets, which come to you in sheep's clothing, but inwardly they are ravening wolves.

16 Ye shall know them by their fruits. Do men gather grapes of thorns, or figs of thistles?

17 Even so, every good tree bringeth forth good fruit; but a corrupt tree bringeth forth evil fruit.

18 A good tree cannot bring forth evil fruit, neither *can* a corrupt tree bring forth good fruit.

19 Every tree that bringeth not forth good fruit is hewn down, and cast into the fire.

20 Wherefore by their fruits ye shall know them.

35 A good man, out of the good treasure of the heart, bringeth forth good things: and an evil man, out of the evil treasure, bringeth forth evil things. M. 12

36 But I say unto you, That every idle word that men shall speak, they shall give account thereof in the day of judgment.

37 For by thy words thou shalt be justified, and by thy words thou shalt be condemned.

24 Therefore whosoever heareth these sayings of mine, and doeth them, I will liken him unto a wise man, which built his house upon a rock: M. 7

25 And the rain descended, and the floods came, and the winds blew, and beat upon that house; and it fell not: for it was founded upon a rock.

26 And every one that heareth these sayings of mine, and doeth them not, shall be likened unto a foolish man, which built his house upon the sand: M. 7.

27 And the rain descended, and the floods came, and the winds blew, and beat upon that house; and it fell, and great was the fall of it.

28 And it came to pass when Jesus had ended these sayings, the people were astonished at his doctrine:

29 For he taught them as *one* having authority, and not as the scribes.

WHEN he was come down from the mountain, great multitudes followed him. M. 8

6. And he went round about the villages, teaching. Mk. 6

28 Come unto me, all *ye* that labour and are heavy laden, and I will give you rest. M. 11

29 Take my yoke upon you, and learn of me; for I am meek and lowly in heart: and ye shall find rest unto your souls.

30 For my yoke *is* easy, and my burden is light.

36 And one of the Pharisees desired him that he would eat with him. And he went into the Pharisee's house, and sat down to meat. L. 7

37 And, behold, a woman in the city, which was a sinner, when she knew that *Jesus* sat at meat in the Pharisee's house, brought an alabaster box of ointment,

38 And stood at his feet behind *him* weeping, and began to wash his feet with tears, and did wipe *them* with the hairs of her head, and kissed his feet, and anointed *them* with the ointment.

39 Now, when the Pharisee which had bidden him saw *it*, he spake within himself, saying, This man, if he were a prophet, would have known who and what manner of woman *this is* that toucheth him; for she is a sinner. L. 7.

40 And Jesus, answering, said unto him, Simon, I have somewhat to say unto thee. And he saith, Master, say on.

41 There was a certain creditor, which had two debtors: the one owed five hundred pence, and the other fifty.

42 And when they had nothing to pay, he frankly forgave them both. Tell me, therefore, which of them will love him most?

43 Simon answered, and said, I suppose that *he* to whom he forgave most. And he said unto him, Thou hast rightly judged.

44 And he turned to the woman, and said unto Simon, Seest thou this woman? I entered into thine house, thou gavest me no water for my feet: but she hath washed my feet with tears, and wiped *them* with the hairs of her head.

45 Thou gavest me no kiss: but this woman, since the time I came in, hath not ceased to kiss my feet.

46 My head with oil thou didst not anoint: but this woman hath anointed my feet with ointment.

31 There came then his brethren and his mother, and, standing without, sent unto him, calling him. Mk. 3.

32 And the multitude sat about him, and they said unto him, Behold, thy mother and thy brethren without seek for thee.

33 And he answered them, saying, Who is my mother, or my brethren?

34 And he looked round about on them which sat about him, and said, Behold my mother and my brethren!

35 For whosoever shall do the will of God, the same is my brother, and my sister, and mother.

IN the mean time, when there were gathered together an innumerable multitude of people, insomuch that they trode one upon another, he began to say unto his disciples first of all, Beware ye of the leaven of the Pharisees, which is hypocrisy.

2 For there is nothing covered, that shall not be revealed; neither hid, that shall not be known.

3 Therefore whatsoever ye have spoken in darkness, shall be heard in the light; and that which ye have spoken in the ear in closets, shall be proclaimed upon the house-tops.

4 And I say unto you, my friends, Be not afraid of them that kill the body, and after that have no more that they can do.

5 But I will forewarn you whom ye shall fear: Fear him, which, after he hath killed, hath power to cast into hell; yea, I say unto you, Fear him.

6 Are not five sparrows sold for two farthings? and not one of them is forgotten before God.

7 But even the very hairs of your head are all numbered. Fear not, therefore; ye are of more value than many sparrows.

13 And one of the company said unto him, Master, speak to my brother, that he divide the inheritance with me.

14 And he said unto him, Man, who made me a judge, or a divider over you?

15 And he said unto them, Take heed, and beware of covetousness; for a man's life consisteth not in the abundance of the things which he possesseth.

16 And he spake a parable unto them, saying, The ground of a certain rich man brought forth plentifully.

17 And he thought within himself, saying, What shall I do, because I have no room where to bestow my fruits?

18 And he said, This will I do: I will pull down my barns, and build greater; and there will I bestow all my fruits and my goods.

19 And I will say to my soul, Soul, thou hast much goods laid up for many years: take thine ease, eat, drink, *and* be merry.

20 But God said unto him, *Thou* fool! this night thy soul shall be required of thee; then whose shall those things be, which thou hast provided?

21 So *is* he that layeth up treasure for himself, and is not rich toward God.

22 And he said unto his disciples, Therefore I say unto you, Take no thought for your life, what ye shall eat; neither for the body, what ye shall put on.

23 The life is more than meat, and the body *is more* than raiment.

24 Consider the ravens: for they neither sow nor reap; which neither have storehouse nor barn; and God feedeth them: How much more are ye better than the fowls?

25 And which of you, with taking thought, can add to his stature one cubit?

26 If ye then be not able to do that thing which is least, why take ye thought for the rest?

27 Consider the lilies how they grow: they toil not, they spin not; and yet I say unto you, That Solomon, in all his glory, was not arrayed like one of these.

28 If then God so clothe the grass, which is to-day in the field, and to-morrow is cast into the oven; how much more *will he clothe* you? O ye of little faith!

29 And seek not ye what ye shall eat, or what ye shall drink; neither be ye of doubtful mind.

30 For all these things do the nations of the world seek after: and your Father knoweth that ye have need of these things.

L. 12.

31 But rather seek ye the king-
dom of God; and all these things
shall be added unto you.

32 Fear not, little flock; for it is
your Father's good pleasure to
give you the kingdom.

33 Sell that ye have, and give
alms; provide yourselves bags
which wax not old, a treasure in
the heavens that faileth not, where
no thief approacheth, neither
moth corrupteth.

34 For where your treasure is,
there will your heart be also.

35 Let your loins be girded
about, and your lights burning:

36 And ye yourselves like unto
men that wait for their lord, when
he will return from the wedding;
that when he cometh and knock-
eth, they may open unto him im-
mediately.

37 Blessed *are* those servants,
whom the lord, when he cometh,
shall find watching: verily I say
unto you, That he shall gird him-
self, and make them to sit down
to meat, and will come forth and
serve them.

38 And if he shall come in the
second watch, or come in the
third watch, and find *them* so,
blessed are those servants.

39 And this know, that if the
good man of the house had known
what hour the thief would come,
he would have watched, and not
have suffered his house to be
broken through.

40 Be ye, therefore, ready also:
for the Son of Man cometh at an
hour when ye think not.

41 Then Peter said unto him,
Lord, speakest thou this parable
unto us, or even to all?

42 And the Lord said, Who then
is that faithful and wise steward,
whom *his* lord shall make ruler
over his household, to give *them*
their portion of meat in due season?

43 Blessed *is* that servant, whom
his lord, when he cometh, shall
find so doing.

L. 12.

44 Of a truth I say unto you,
That he will make him ruler over
all that he hath.

45 But, and if that servant say in
his heart, My lord delayeth his
coming; and shall begin to beat the
men-servants, and maidens, and to
eat and drink, and to be drunken;

46 The lord of that servant will
come in a day when he looketh
not for *him*, and at an hour when
he is not aware, and will cut him
in sunder.

47 And that servant, which knew
his lord's will, and prepared not
himself, neither did according to
his will, shall be beaten with ma-
ny *stripes*.

48 But he that knew not, and did
commit things worthy of stripes,
shall be beaten with few *stripes*.
For unto whomsoever much is
given, of him shall be much re-
quired: and to whom men have
committed much, of him they will
ask the more.

54 And he said also to the people,
When ye see a cloud rise out of
the west, straightway ye say, There
cometh a shower, and so it is.

55 And when *ye see* the south
wind blow, ye say, There will be
heat; and it cometh to pass.

56 Ye hypocrites! ye can dis-
cern the face of the sky and of the
earth; but how is it, that ye do
not discern this time?

57 Yea, and why even of your-
selves judge ye not what is right?

58 When thou goest with thine
adversary to the magistrate, *as*
thou art in the way, give diligence
that thou mayest be delivered
from him; lest he hale thee to
the judge, and the judge deliver
thee to the officer, and the officer
cast thee into prison.

59 I tell thee, thou shalt not de-
part thence, till thou hast paid the
very last mite.

THERE were present at that season some that told him of the Galileans, whose blood Pilate had mingled with their sacrifices. L. 13

2 And Jesus, answering, said unto them, Suppose ye that these Galileans were sinners above all the Galileans, because they suffered such things?

3 I tell you, Nay; but, except ye repent, ye shall all likewise perish.

4 Or those eighteen upon whom the tower in Siloam fell, and slew them, think ye that they were sinners above all men that dwelt in Jerusalem?

5 I tell you, Nay; but except ye repent, ye shall all likewise perish.

6 He spake also this parable: A certain *man* had a fig-tree planted in his vineyard; and he came and sought fruit thereon, and found none.

7 Then said he unto the dresser of his vineyard, Behold, these three years I come seeking fruit on this fig-tree, and find none: cut it down; why cumbereth it the ground?

8 And he, answering, said unto him, Lord, let it alone this year also, till I shall dig about it, and dung *it*:

9 And if it bear fruit, *well*: and if not, *then* after that thou shalt cut it down.

37 And as he spake, a certain Pharisee besought him to dine with him: and he went in, and sat down to meat. L. 11.

38 And when the Pharisee saw *it*, he marvelled that he had not first washed before dinner.

39 And the Lord said unto him, Now do ye Pharisees make clean the outside of the cup and the platter; but your inward part is full of ravening and wickedness.

40 *Ye* fools! did not he that made that which is without, make that which is within also?

41 But rather give alms of such things as ye have; and, behold, all things are clean unto you.

42 But woe unto you, Pharisees! for ye tithe mint, and rue, and all manner of herbs, and pass over judgment and the love of God: these ought ye to have done, and not to leave the other undone. L. 1

43 Woe unto you, Pharisees! for ye love the uppermost seats in the synagogues, and greetings in the markets.

44 Woe unto you, scribes and Pharisees, hypocrites! for ye are as graves which appear not, and the men that walk over *them* are not aware *of them*.

45 Then answered one of the lawyers, and said unto him, Master, thus saying, thou reproachest us also.

46 And he said, Woe unto you also, *ye* lawyers! for ye lade men with burdens grievous to be borne, and ye yourselves touch not the burdens with one of your fingers.

52 Woe unto you, lawyers! for ye have taken away the key of knowledge: ye entered not in yourselves, and them that were entering in ye hindered.

53 And as he said these things unto them, the scribes and the Pharisees began to urge *him* vehemently, and to provoke him to speak of many things; I 2

54 Laying wait for him, and seeking to catch something out of his mouth, that they might accuse him

THE same day went Jesus out of the house, and sat by the sea side. M. 13

2 And great multitudes were gathered together unto him, so that he went into a ship and sat; and the whole multitude stood on the shore.

3 And he spake many things unto them in parables, saying, Behold, a sower went forth to sow;

4 And, when he sowed, some *seeds* fell by the way-side, and the fowls came and devoured them

M. 13.

5 Some fell upon stony places, where they had not much earth: and forthwith they sprung up, because they had no deepness of earth:

6 And when the sun was up, they were scorched: and, because they had not root, they withered away.

7 And some fell among thorns; and the thorns sprung up and choked them:

8 But other fell into good ground, and brought forth fruit, some an hundred-fold, some sixty-fold, some thirty-fold.

9 Who hath ears to hear, let him hear.

Mk. 4.

10 And when he was alone, they that were about him, with the twelve, asked of him the parable.

M. 13

18 Hear ye, therefore, the parable of the sower.

19 When any one heareth the word of the kingdom, and understandeth *it* not, *then* cometh the wicked *one*, and catcheth away that which was sown in his heart. This is he which received seed by the way *side*.

20 But he that received the seed into stony places, the same is he that heareth the word, and anon with joy receiveth it;

21 Yet hath he not root in himself, but dureth for a while; for when tribulation or persecution ariseth because of the word, by and by he is offended.

22 He also that received seed among the thorns, is he that heareth the word; and the care of this world, and the deceitfulness of riches, choke the word, and he becometh unfruitful.

23 But he that received seed into the good ground, is he that heareth the word and understandeth *it*; which also beareth fruit, and bringeth forth, some an hundred-fold, some sixty, some thirty.

Mk. 4.

21 And he said unto them, Is a candle brought to be put under a bushel, or under a bed, and not to be set on a candlestick?

22 For there is nothing hid which shall not be manifested; neither was any thing kept secret, but that it should come abroad.

23 If any man have ears to hear, let him hear.

M. 13

24 Another parable put he forth unto them, saying, The kingdom of heaven is likened unto a man which sowed good seed in his field:

25 But, while men slept, his enemy came and sowed tares among the wheat, and went his way.

26 But when the blade was sprung up, and brought forth fruit, then appeared the tares also.

27 So the servants of the householder came and said unto him, Sir, didst not thou sow good seed in thy field? from whence then hath it tares?

28 He said unto them, An enemy hath done this. The servants said unto him, Wilt thou then that we go and gather them up?

29 But he said, Nay; lest, while ye gather up the tares, ye root up also the wheat with them.

30 Let both grow together until the harvest; and in the time of harvest I will say to the reapers, Gather ye together first the tares, and bind them in bundles to burn them: but gather the wheat into my barn.

36 Then Jesus sent the multitude away, and went into the house: and his disciples came unto him, saying, Declare unto us the parable of the tares of the field.

37 He answered and said unto them, He that soweth the good seed is the Son of Man;

38 The field is the world; the good seed are the children of the kingdom; but the tares are the children of the wicked *one*;

Mt. 13

39 The enemy that sowed them is the devil: the harvest is the end of the world: and the reapers are the angels.

40 As, therefore, the tares are gathered and burned in the fire; so shall it be in the end of this world.

41 The Son of Man shall send forth his angels, and they shall gather out of his kingdom all things that offend, and them which do iniquity;

42 And shall cast them into a furnace of fire: there shall be wailing and gnashing of teeth.

43 Then shall the righteous shine forth as the sun in the kingdom of their Father. Who hath ears to hear, let him hear.

44 Again, the kingdom of heaven is like unto treasure hid in a field; the which when a man hath found he hideth, and, for joy thereof, goeth and selleth all that he hath, and buyeth that field.

45 Again, the kingdom of heaven is like unto a merchantman, seeking goodly pearls:

46 Who, when he had found one pearl of great price, went and sold all that he had, and bought it.

47 Again, the kingdom of heaven is like unto a net, that was cast into the sea, and gathered of every kind:

48 Which, when it was full, they drew to shore, and sat down, and gathered the good into vessels, but cast the bad away.

49 So shall it be at the end of the world: the angels shall come forth, and sever the wicked from among the just.

50 And shall cast them into the furnace of fire: there shall be wailing and gnashing of teeth.

51 Jesus saith unto them, Have ye understood all these things? They say unto him, Yea, Lord.

52 Then said he unto them, Therefore every scribe *which is* instructed unto the kingdom of heaven is like unto a man *that is* an householder, which bringeth forth out of his treasure *things* new and old.

Mk.

26 And he said, So is the kingdom of God, as if a man should cast seed into the ground;

27 And should sleep, and rise night and day, and the seed should spring and grow up, he knoweth not how.

28 For the earth bringeth forth fruit of herself; first the blade, then the ear, after that the full corn in the ear.

29 But when the fruit is brought forth, immediately he putteth in the sickle, because the harvest is come.

30 And he said, Whereunto shall we liken the kingdom of God? or with what comparison shall we compare it?

31 *It is* like a grain of mustard-seed, which, when it is sown in the earth, is less than all the seeds that be in the earth:

32 But when it is sown, it groweth up, and becometh greater than all herbs, and shooteth out great branches; so that the fowls of the air may lodge under the shadow of it.

33 And with many such parables spake he the word unto them, as they were able to hear *it*.

34 But without a parable spake he not unto them: and when they were alone, he expounded all things to his disciples.

L. 9

57 And it came to pass, that, as they went in the way, a certain *man* said unto him, Lord, I will follow thee whithersoever thou goest.

58 And Jesus said unto him, Foxes have holes, and birds of the air *have* nests; but the Son of Man hath not where to lay *his* head.

59 And he said unto another, Follow me. But he said, Lord, suffer me first to go and bury my father.

60 Jesus said unto him, Let the dead bury their dead: but go thou and preach the kingdom of God.

61 And another also said, Lord, I will follow thee: but let me first go bid them farewell, which are at home at my house.

62 And Jesus said unto him, No man having put his hand to the plough, and looking back, is fit for the kingdom of God.

27 And after these things, he went forth, and saw a publican, named Levi, sitting at the receipt of custom: and he said unto him, Follow me. L. 5.

28 And he left all, rose up, and followed him.

29 And Levi made him a great feast in his own house: and 15 many publicans and sinners sat also together with Jesus and his disciples: for there were many, and they followed him. Mk. 2.

16 And when the scribes and Pharisees saw him eat with publicans and sinners, they said unto his disciples, How is it that he eateth and drinketh with publicans and sinners?

17 When Jesus heard *it*, he saith unto them, They that are whole have no need of the physician, but they that are sick: I came not to call the righteous, but sinners to repentance.

36 And he spake also a parable unto them; No man putteth a piece of a new garment upon an old; if otherwise, then both the new maketh a rent, and the piece that was *taken* out of the new agreeth not with the old. L. 5.

37 And no man putteth new wine into old bottles; else the new wine will burst the bottles, and be spilled, and the bottles shall perish.

38 But new wine must be put into new bottles; and both are preserved.

53 And it came to pass, *that* when Jesus had finished these parables, he departed thence. M. 13.

54 And when he was come into his own country, he taught them in their synagogue, insomuch that they were astonished, and said, Whence hath this *man* this wisdom, and *these* mighty works?

55 Is not this the carpenter's son? is not his mother called Mary? and his brethren, James, and Joses, and Simon, and Judas?

56 And his sisters, are they not all with us? Whence then hath this *man* all these things? M. 13.

57 And they were offended in him. But Jesus said unto them, A prophet is not without honour, save in his own country, and in his own house.

36 But when he saw the multitudes, he was moved with compassion on them, because they fainted, and were scattered abroad, as sheep having no shepherd. M. 9.

7 And he calleth *unto him* the twelve, and began to send them forth by two and two; Mk. 6.

and commanded them, saying, Go not into the way of the Gentiles, and into *any* city of the Samaritans enter ye not: M. 10.

6 But go rather to the lost sheep of the house of Israel.

9 Provide neither gold, nor silver, nor brass in your purses;

10 Nor scrip for your journey, neither two coats, neither shoes, nor yet staves: for the workman is worthy of his meat.

11 And into whatsoever city or town ye shall enter, enquire who in it is worthy; and there abide till ye go thence.

12 And when ye come into an house, salute it.

13 And if the house be worthy, let your peace come upon it: but if it be not worthy, let your peace return to you.

14 And whosoever shall not receive you, nor hear your words, when ye depart out of that house, or city, shake off the dust of your feet.

15 Verily I say unto you, It shall be more tolerable for the land of Sodom and Gomorrha, in the day of judgment, than for that city.

16 Behold, I send you forth as sheep in the midst of wolves: be ye, therefore, wise as serpents, and harmless as doves.

17 But beware of men: for they will deliver you up to the councils, and they will scourge you

Mt. 10.

in their synagogues:

18 And ye shall be brought before governors and kings for my sake, for a testimony against them and the Gentiles.

23 But when they persecute you in this city, flee ye into another:

26 Fear them not, therefore: for there is nothing covered, that shall not be revealed; and hid, that shall not be known.

27 What I tell you in darkness, *that* speak ye in light: and what ye hear in the ear, *that* preach ye upon the housetops.

28 And fear not them which kill the body, but are not able to kill the soul: but rather fear him which is able to destroy both soul and body in hell.

29 Are not two sparrows sold for a farthing? and one of them shall not fall on the ground without your Father.

30 But the very hairs of your head are all numbered.

31 Fear ye not, therefore, ye are of more value than many sparrows.

Mk. 6.

12 And they went out, and preached that men should repent.

30 And the apostles gathered themselves together unto Jesus, and told him all things, both what they had done, and what they had taught.

J. 7.

AFTER these things Jesus walked in Galilee: for he would not walk in Jewry, because the Jews sought to kill him.

Mk. 7.

THEN came together unto him, the Pharisees, and certain of the scribes, which came from Jerusalem.

2 And when they saw some of his disciples eat bread with defiled (that is to say, with unwashen) hands, they found fault.

3 For the Pharisees, and all the Jews, except they wash *their* hands oft, eat not, holding the tradition of the elders.

4 And *when they come* from the market, except they wash, they eat not. And many other things there be, which they have received to hold, *as* the washing of cups, and pots, and of brasen vessels, and tables.

5 Then the Pharisees and scribes asked him, Why walk not thy disciples according to the tradition of the elders, but eat bread with unwashen hands?

14 And, when he had called all the people *unto him*, he said unto them, Hearken unto me every one *of you*, and understand:

15 There is nothing from without a man, that entering into him can defile him: but the things which come out of him, those are they that defile the man.

16 If any man have ears to hear, let him hear.

17 And, when he was entered into the house from the people, his disciples asked him concerning the parable.

18 And he saith unto them, Are ye so without understanding also? Do ye not perceive, that whatsoever thing from without entereth into the man, *it* cannot defile him;

19 Because it entereth not into his heart, but into the belly, and goeth out into the draught, purging all meats?

20 And he said, That which cometh out of the man, that defileth the man.

21 For from within, out of the heart of men, proceed evil thoughts, adulteries, fornications, murders,

22 Thefts, covetousness, wickedness, deceit, lasciviousness, an evil eye, blasphemy, pride, foolishness:

23 All these evil things come from within, and defile the man.

24 And from thence he arose, and went into the borders of Tyre and Sidon, and entered into an house, and would have no man know *it*: but he could not be hid,

M. 18

AT the same time came the disciples unto Jesus, saying, Who is the greatest in the kingdom of heaven?

2 And Jesus called a little child unto him, and set him in the midst of them,

3 And said, Verily I say unto you, Except ye be converted, and become as little children, ye shall not enter into the kingdom of heaven.

4 Whosoever, therefore, shall humble himself as this little child, the same is greatest in the kingdom of heaven.

7 Woe unto the world because of offences! for it must needs be that offences come; but woe to that man by whom the offence cometh!

8 Wherefore, if thy hand or thy foot offend thee, cut them off, and cast *them* from thee: it is better for thee to enter into life halt or maimed, rather than having two hands, or two feet, to be cast into everlasting fire

9 And if thine eye offend thee, pluck it out, and cast *it* from thee: it is better for thee to enter into life with one eye, rather than having two eyes to be cast into hell-fire.

12 How think ye? if a man have an hundred sheep, and one of them be gone astray, doth he not leave the ninety and nine, and goeth into the mountains, and seeketh that which is gone astray?

13 And if so be that he find it, verily I say unto you, He rejoiceth more of that *sheep*, than of the ninety and nine which went not astray.

14 Even so it is not the will of your Father which is in heaven, that one of these little ones should perish.

15 Moreover, if thy brother shall trespass against thee, go and tell him his fault between thee and him alone: if he shall hear thee, thou hast gained thy brother.

M. 18

16 But if he will not hear *thee*, *then* take with thee one or two more, that in the mouth of two or three witnesses every word may be established.

17 And if he shall neglect to hear them, tell *it* unto the church: but if he neglect to hear the church, let him be unto thee as an heathen man and a publican.

21 Then came Peter to him, and said, Lord, how oft shall my brother sin against me, and I forgive him? till seven times?

22 Jesus saith unto him, I say not unto thee, Until seven times; but, Until seventy times seven.

23 Therefore is the kingdom of heaven likened unto a certain king, which would take account of his servants.

24 And when he had begun to reckon, one was brought unto him, which owed him ten thousand talents.

25 But forasmuch as he had not to pay, his lord commanded him to be sold, and his wife, and children, and all that he had, and payment to be made.

26 The servant, therefore fell down, and worshipped him, saying, lord, have patience with me, and I will pay thee all.

27 Then the lord of that servant was moved with compassion, and loosed him, and forgave him the debt.

28 But the same servant went out, and found one of his fellow-servants, which owed him an hundred pence: and he laid hands on him, and took *him* by the throat, saying, Pay me that thou owest.

29 And his fellow-servant fell down at his feet, and besought him, saying, Have patience with me, and I will pay thee all.

30 And he would not: but went and cast him into prison, till he should pay the debt.

M. 18

31 So when his fellow-servants saw what was done, they were very sorry, and came and told unto their lord all that was done.

32 Then his lord, after that he had called him, said unto him, O thou wicked servant! I forgave thee all that debt, because thou desiredst me:

33 Shouldest not thou also have had compassion on thy fellow-servant, even as I had pity on thee?

34 And his lord was wroth, and delivered him to the tormentors, till he should pay all that was due unto him.

35 So likewise shall my heavenly Father do also unto you, if ye from your hearts forgive not every one his brother their trespasses.

L. 10

AFTER these things the Lord appointed other seventy also, and sent them two and two before his face into every city and place, whither he himself would come.

2 Therefore said he unto them, The harvest truly *is* great, but the labourers *are* few: pray ye therefore the lord of the harvest, that he would send forth labourers into his harvest.

3 Go your ways: behold, I send you forth as lambs among wolves.

4 Carry neither purse, nor scrip, nor shoes: and salute no man by the way.

5 And into whatsoever house ye enter, first say, Peace *be* to this house.

6 And if the Son of Peace be there, your peace shall rest upon it: if not, it shall turn to you again.

7 And in the same house remain, eating and drinking such things as they give: for the labourer is worthy of his hire. Go not from house to house.

8 And into whatsoever city ye enter, and they receive you, eat such things as are set before you;

L. 1

10 But into whatsoever city ye enter, and they receive you not, go your ways out into the streets of the same, and say,

11 Even the very dust of your city, which cleaveth on us, we do wipe off against you: notwithstanding, be ye sure of this, that the kingdom of God is come nigh unto you.

12 But I say unto you, That it shall be more tolerable in that day for Sodom, than for that city.

J. 7

2 Now the Jews' feast of tabernacles was at hand.

3 His brethren, therefore, said unto him, Depart hence, and go into Judea, that thy disciples also may see the works that thou doest.

4 For *there is* no man *that* doeth any thing in secret, and he himself seeketh to be known openly. If thou do these things, shew thyself to the world.

5 For neither did his brethren believe in him.

6 Then Jesus said unto them, My time is not yet come: but your time is alway ready.

7 The world cannot hate you: but me it hateth, because I testify of it, that the works thereof are evil.

8 Go ye up unto this feast: I go not up yet unto this feast; for my time is not yet full come.

9 When he had said these words unto them, he abode *still* in Galilee.

10 But when his brethren were gone up, then went he also up unto the feast, not openly, but as it were in secret.

11 Then the Jews sought him at the feast, and said, Where is he?

12 And there was much murmuring among the people concerning him: for some said, He is a good man: others said, Nay; but he deceiveth the people.

13 Howbeit no man spake openly of him for fear of the Jews.

14 Now, about the midst of the feast, Jesus went up into the temple, and taught.

15 And the Jews marvelled, saying, How knoweth this man letters, having never learned?

16 Jesus answered them, and said,

J. 7.

19 Did not Moses give you the law,
and *yet* none of you keepeth the
law? Why go ye about to kill me?
20 The people answered, and
said, Thou hast a devil: who go-
eth about to kill thee?
21 Jesus answered, and said un-
to them, I have done one work,
and ye all marvel.
22 Moses, therefore, gave unto
you circumcision, (not because it
is of Moses, but of the fathers,)
and ye on the sabbath-day cir-
cumcise a man.
23 If a man on the sabbath-day
receive circumcision, that the law
of Moses should not be broken;
are ye angry at me, because I have
made a man every whit whole on
the sabbath-day?
24 Judge not according to the
appearance, but judge righteous
judgment.
25 Then said some of them of
Jerusalem, Is not this he whom
they seek to kill?
26 But, lo, he speaketh boldly,
and they say nothing unto him;
Do the rulers know indeed that
this is the very Christ?
32 The Pharisees heard that the
people murmured such things
concerning him; and the Phari-
sees, and the chief priest sent
officers to take him.
43 So there was a division among
the people because of him.
44 And some of them would
have taken him; but no man laid
hands on him.
45 Then came the officers to the
chief priests and Pharisees; and
they said unto them, Why have
ye not brought him? M 2.
46 The officers answered, Never
man spake like this man.
47 Then answered them the Pha-
sees, Are ye also deceived?
8 Have any of the rulers, or of
e Pharisees, believed on him?
9 But this people who knoweth
t the law are cursed.

0 Nicodemus saith unto them,
e that came to Jesus by night,
eing one of them,)
1 Doth our law judge *any* man,
efore it hear him, and know what
e doeth?
52 They answered, and said un-
him, Art thou also of Galilee?
earch, and look: for out of Ga-
lee ariseth no prophet.
53 And every man went unto his
wn house.

J. 8.

JESUS went unto the mount of
Olives.
2 And early in the morning he
ame again into the temple, and
ll the people came unto him:
nd he sat down, and taught them.
3 And the scribes and Pharisees
rought unto him a woman taken
i adultery; and, when they had
et her in the midst,
4 They say unto him, Master,
his woman was taken in adulte-
y, in the very act.
5 Now Moses in the law com-
nanded us, That such should be
toned: but what sayest thou?
6 This they said, tempting him,
that they might have to accuse
him. But Jesus stooped down,
and with *his* finger wrote on the
ground, *as though he heard them*
not.
7 So, when they continued ask-
ing him, he lifted up himself, and
said unto them, He that is with-
out sin among you, let him first
cast a stone at her.
8 And again he stooped down,
and wrote on the ground.
9 And they which heard *it*, be-
ing convicted by *their own* con-
science, went out one by one, be-
ginning at the eldest, *even* unto the
last; and Jesus was left alone, and
the woman standing in the midst.
10 When Jesus had lifted up him-
self, and saw none but the wo-
man, he said unto her, Woman,
where are those thine accusers?
hath no man condemned thee?
11 She said, No man, Lord. And
Jesus said unto her, Neither do I
condemn thee: go, and sin no more.

J. 9.

AND as *Jesus* passed by, he saw a man which was blind from *his* birth.

2 And his disciples asked him, saying, Master, who did sin, this man, or his parents, that he was born blind?

3 Jesus answered, Neither hath this man sinned, nor his parents: but that the works of God should be made manifest in him.

J. 10.

VERILY, verily, I say unto you, He that entereth not by the door into the sheep-fold, but climbeth up some other way, the same is a thief and a robber.

2 But he that entereth in by the door, is the shepherd of the sheep.

3 To him the porter openeth; and the sheep hear his voice: and he calleth his own sheep by name, and leadeth them out.

4 And when he putteth forth his own sheep, he goeth before them, and the sheep follow him: for they know his voice.

5 And a stranger will they not follow, but will flee from him: for they know not the voice of strangers.

11 I am the good shepherd: the good shepherd giveth his life for the sheep.

12 But he that is an hireling, and not the shepherd, whose own the sheep are not, seeth the wolf coming, and leaveth the sheep, and fleeth: and the wolf catcheth them, and scattereth the sheep.

13 The hireling fleeth, because he is an hireling, and careth not for the sheep.

14 I am the good shepherd, and know my *sheep*, and am known of mine.

16 And other sheep I have, which are not of this fold: them also I must bring, and they shall hear my voice; and there shall be one fold, *and* one shepherd.

L.

25 And, behold, a certain lawyer stood up, and tempted him, saying, Master, what shall I do to inherit eternal life?

26 He said unto him, What is written in the law? how readest thou?

27 And he answering, said, Thou shalt love the Lord thy God with all thy heart, and with all thy soul, and with all thy strength, and with all thy mind; and thy neighbour as thyself.

28 And he said unto him, Thou hast answered right: this do, and thou shalt live.

29 But he, willing to justify himself, said unto Jesus, And who is my neighbour?

30 And Jesus, answering, said, A certain *man* went down from Jerusalem to Jericho, and fell among thieves, which stripped him of his raiment, and wounded *him*, and departed, leaving *him* half dead.

31 And, by chance, there came down a certain priest that way; and when he saw him, he passed by on the other side.

32 And likewise a Levite, when he was at the place, came and looked *on him*, and passed by on the other side.

33 But a certain Samaritan, as he journeyed, came where he was: and when he saw him, he had compassion *on him*.

34 And went to *him*, and bound up his wounds, pouring in oil and wine, and set him on his own beast, and brought him to an inn, and took care of him.

35 And on the morrow, when he departed, he took out two pence, and gave *them* to the host, and said unto him, Take care of him: and whatsoever thou spendest more, when I come again, I will repay thee.

36 Which now of these three, thinkest thou was neighbour unto him that fell among the thieves?

37 And he said, He that shewed mercy on him. Then said Jesus unto him, Go, and do thou likewise.

L. 11.

AND it came to pass, that, as
he was praying in a certain
place, when he ceased, one of his
disciples said unto him, Lord,
teach us to pray, as John also
taught his disciples.
2 And he said unto them, When
ye pray, say, Our Father, which
art in heaven: Hallowed be thy
name. Thy kingdom come. Thy
will be done, as in heaven, so in
earth.
3 Give us day by day our daily
bread.
4 And forgive us our sins; for
we also forgive every one that is
indebted to us. And lead us not
into temptation; but deliver us
from evil.
5 And he said unto them, Which
of you shall have a friend, and
shall go unto him at midnight,
and say unto him, Friend, lend
me three loaves;
6 For a friend of mine in his
journey is come to me, and I have
nothing to set before him?
7 And he from within shall an-
swer, and say, Trouble me not:
the door is now shut, and my
children are with me in bed; I
cannot rise and give thee.
8 I say unto you, Though he will
not rise and give him, because he
is his friend; yet because of his
importunity he will rise and give
him as many as he needeth.
9 And I say unto you, Ask, and
it shall be given you; seek, and
ye shall find: knock, and it shall
be opened unto you.
10 For every one that asketh, re-
ceiveth: and he that seeketh, find-
eth; and to him that knocketh, it
shall be opened.
11 If a son shall ask bread of any
of you that is a father, will he give
him a stone? or, if *he ask* a fish,
will he for a fish give him a ser-
pent?
12 Or, if he shall ask an egg,
will he offer him a scorpion?

L. 11.

13 If ye then, being evil, know
how to give good gifts unto your
children; how much more shall
your heavenly Father give the Ho-
ly Spirit to them that ask him?

L. 14.

AND it came to pass, as he
went into the house of one
of the chief Pharisees to eat bread
on the sabbath-day, that they
watched him.
2 And, behold, there was a cer-
tain man before him, which had
the dropsy.
3 And Jesus, answering, spake
unto the lawyers and Pharisees,
saying, Is it lawful to heal on the
sabbath-day?
4 And they held their peace.
5 (And he saith unto them,) Which of you shall have an ass
or an ox fallen into a pit, and will
not straightway pull him out on
the sabbath-day?
6 And they could not answer him
again to these things.
7 And he put forth a parable to
those which were bidden, when
he marked how they chose out the
chief rooms; saying unto them,
8 When thou art bidden of any
man to a wedding, sit not down in
the highest room; lest a more ho-
nourable man than thou be bidden
of him;
9 And he that bade thee and him,
come and say to thee, Give this
man place; and thou begin with
shame to take the lowest room.
10 But when thou art bidden, go
and sit down in the lowest room;
that when he that bade thee com-
eth, he may say unto thee, Friend,
go up higher: then shalt thou
have worship in the presence of
them that sit at meat with thee.
11 For whosoever exalteth him-
self shall be abased; and he that
humbleth himself shall be exalted.
12 Then said he also to him that
bade him, When thou makest a
dinner or a supper, call not thy
friends, nor thy brethren, neither
thy kinsmen, nor thy rich neigh-
bours; lest they also bid thee again,
and a recompense be made thee.

L. 14

13 But when thou makest a feast, call the poor, the maimed, the lame, the blind:

14 And thou shalt be blessed; for they cannot recompense thee: for thou shalt be recompensed at the resurrection of the just.

16 Then said he unto him, A certain man made a great supper, and bade many:

17 And sent his servant at supper-time to say to them that were bidden, Come, for all things are now ready.

18 And they all with one *consent* began to make excuse. The first said unto him, I have bought a piece of ground, and I must needs go and see it: I pray thee have me excused.

19 And another said, I have bought five yoke of oxen, and I go to prove them: I pray thee have me excused.

20 And another said, I have married a wife; and therefore I cannot come.

21 So that servant came, and shewed his lord these things. Then the master of the house, being angry, said to his servant, Go out quickly into the streets and lanes of the city, and bring in hither the poor, and the maimed, and the halt, and the blind.

22 And the servant said, Lord, it is done as thou hast commanded, and yet there is room.

23 And the lord said unto the servant, Go out into the highways and hedges, and compel *them* to come in, that my house may be filled.

24 For I say unto you, That none of those men which were bidden, shall taste of my supper.

28 For which of you, intending to build a tower, sitteth not down first, and counteth the cost, whether he have *sufficient* to finish *it?*

29 Lest haply, after he hath laid the foundation, and is not able to finish *it*, all that behold *it* begin to mock him,

30 Saying, This man began to build, and was not able to finish.

31 Or what king, going to make war against another king, sitteth not down first, and consulteth whether he be able with ten thousand to meet him that cometh against him with twenty thousand?

32 Or else, while the other is yet a great way off, he sendeth an ambassage, and desireth conditions of peace.

L. 1

THEN drew near unto him all the publicans and sinners for to hear him.

2 And the Pharisees and scribes murmured, saying, This man receiveth sinners, and eateth with them.

3 And he spake this parable unto them, saying,

4 What man of you, having an hundred sheep, if he lose one of them, doth not leave the ninety and nine in the wilderness, and go after that which is lost, until he find it?

5 And when he hath found *it*, he layeth *it* on his shoulders, rejoicing.

6 And when he cometh home, he calleth together *his* friends and neighbours, saying unto them, Rejoice with me; for I have found my sheep which was lost.

7 I say unto you, That likewise joy shall be in heaven over one sinner that repenteth, more than over ninety and nine just persons, which need no repentance.

8 Either what woman, having ten pieces of silver, if she lose one piece, doth not light a candle, and sweep the house, and seek diligently till she find *it?*

9 And when she hath found *it*, she calleth *her* friends and *her* neighbours together, saying, Rejoice with me; for I have found the piece which I had lost.

10 Likewise, I say unto you, There is joy in the presence of the angels of God, over one sinner that repenteth.

11 And he said, A certain man had two sons: L. 15

12 And the younger of them said to *his* father, Father, give me the portion of goods that falleth *to me*. And he divided unto them *his* living.

13 And not many days after the younger son gathered all together, and took his journey into a far country, and there wasted his substance with riotous living.

14 And when he had spent all, there arose a mighty famine in that land; and he began to be in want.

15 And he went and joined himself to a citizen of that country; and he sent him into his fields to feed swine.

16 And he would fain have filled his belly with the husks that the swine did eat: and no man gave unto him.

17 And when he came to himself, he said, How many hired servants of my father's have bread enough, and to spare, and I perish with hunger!

18 I will arise, and go to my father, and will say unto him, Father, I have sinned against heaven, and before thee,

19 And am no more worthy to be called thy son: make me as one of thy hired servants.

20 And he arose, and came to his father. But, when he was yet a great way off, his father saw him, and had compassion, and ran, and fell on his neck, and kissed him.

21 And the son said unto him, Father, I have sinned against heaven, and in thy sight, and am no more worthy to be called thy son.

22 But the father said to his servants, Bring forth the best robe, and put *it* on him; and put a ring on his hand, and shoes on *his* feet:

23 And bring hither the fatted calf, and kill *it*; and let us eat, and be merry:

24 For this my son was dead, and is alive again; he was lost, and is found. And they began to be merry. L. 15.

25 Now, his elder son was in the field: and as he came and drew nigh to the house, he heard musick and dancing.

26 And he called one of the servants, and asked what these things meant.

27 And he said unto him, Thy brother is come; and thy father hath killed the fatted calf, because he hath received him safe and sound.

28 And he was angry, and would not go in: therefore came his father out, and entreated him.

29 And he, answering, said to *his* father, Lo, these many years do I serve thee, neither transgressed I at any time thy commandment; and yet thou never gavest me a kid, that I might make merry with my friends:

30 But as soon as this thy son was come, which hath devoured thy living with harlots, thou hast killed for him the fatted calf.

31 And he said unto him, Son, thou art ever with me, and all that I have is thine.

32 It was meet that we should make merry, and be glad: for this thy brother was dead, and is alive again; and was lost, and is found.

CHAP. XVI. L.

Of the unjust steward.

AND he said also unto his disciples, There was a certain rich man, which had a steward; and the same was accused unto him that he had wasted his goods.

2 And he called him, and said unto him, How is it that I hear this of thee? give an account of thy stewardship; for thou mayest be no longer steward.

3 Then the steward said within himself, What shall I do, for my lord taketh away from me the stewardship? I cannot dig; to beg I am ashamed.

4 I am resolved what to do, that when I am put out of the stewardship, they may receive me into their houses.

5 So he called every one of his lord's debtors *unto him*, and said unto the first, How much owest thou unto my lord?

6 And he said, An hundred measures of oil. And he said unto him, Take thy bill, and sit down quickly, and write fifty.

7 Then said he to another, And how much owest thou? And he said, An hundred measures of wheat. And he said unto him, Take thy bill, and write fourscore.

8 And the lord commended the unjust steward, because he had done wisely: for the children of this world are in their generation wiser than the children of light.

9 And I say unto you, Make to yourselves friends of the mammon of unrighteousness; that, when ye fail, they may receive you into everlasting habitations.

10 He that is faithful in that which is least, is faithful also in much; and he that is unjust in the least, is unjust also in much.

11 If, therefore, ye have not been faithful in the unrighteous mammon, who will commit to your trust the true *riches*?

12 And if ye have not been faithful in that which is another man's, who shall give you that which is your own?

13 No servant can serve two masters: for either he will hate the one, and love the other; or else he will hold to the one, and despise the other. Ye cannot serve God and mammon.

14 And the Pharisees also, who were covetous, heard all these things: and they derided him.

15 And he said unto them, Ye are they which justify yourselves before men; but God knoweth your hearts: for that which is highly esteemed among men is abomination in the sight of God.

18 Whosoever putteth away his wife, and marrieth another, committeth adultery: and whosoever marrieth her that is put away from *her* husband, committeth adultery.

19 There was a certain rich man, which was clothed in purple and fine linen, and fared sumptuously every day:

20 And there was a certain beggar, named Lazarus, which was laid at his gate full of sores,

21 And desiring to be fed with the crumbs which fell from the rich man's table: moreover, the dogs came and licked his sores.

22 And it came to pass, that the beggar died, and was carried by the angels into Abraham's bosom: the rich man also died, and was buried;

23 And in hell he lifted up his eyes, being in torments, and seeth Abraham afar off, and Lazarus in his bosom.

24 And he cried, and said, Father Abraham, have mercy on me; and send Lazarus, that he may dip the tip of his finger in water, and cool my tongue; for I am tormented in this flame.

25 But Abraham said, Son, remember that thou in thy life time receivedst thy good things, and likewise Lazarus evil things: but now he is comforted, and thou art tormented.

26 And, besides all this, between us and you there is a great gulf fixed: so that they which would pass from hence to you cannot; neither can they pass to us, that *would come* from thence.

27 Then he said, I pray thee, therefore, father, that thou wouldest send him to my father's house:

28 For I have five brethren; that he may testify unto them, lest they also come into this place of torment.

29 Abraham saith unto him, They have Moses and the prophets; let them hear them.

L. 16.

30 And he said, Nay, father Abraham: but if one went unto them from the dead, they will repent.

31 And he said unto him, If they hear not Moses and the prophets, neither will they be persuaded though one rose from the dead.

L.

CHAP. XVII.

To avoid giving offence.

THEN said he unto the disciples, It is impossible but that offences will come: but woe *unto him* through whom they come?

2 It were better for him that a mill-stone were hanged about his neck, and he cast into the sea, than that he should offend one of these little ones.

3 Take heed to yourselves: If thy brother trespass against thee, rebuke him; and if he repent, forgive him.

4 And if he trespass against thee seven times in a day, and seven times in a day turn again to thee, saying, I repent; thou shalt forgive him.

7 But which of you having a servant plowing, or feeding cattle, will say unto him by and by, when he is come from the field, Go and sit down to meat?

8 And will not rather say unto him, Make ready wherewith I may sup, and gird thyself, and serve me, till I have eaten and drunken; and afterward thou shalt eat and drink?

9 Doth he thank that servant because he did the things that were commanded him? I trow not.

10 So likewise ye, when ye shall have done all those things which are commanded you, say, We are unprofitable servants: we have done that which was our duty to do.

20 And when he was demanded of the Pharisees, when the kingdom of God should come, he answered them, and said, The kingdom of God cometh not with observation.

L. 17.

26 And as it was in the days of Noe, so shall it be also in the days of the Son of Man:

27 They did eat, they drank, they married wives, they were given in marriage, until the day that Noe entered into the ark; and the flood came, and destroyed them all.

28 Likewise also, as it was in the days of Lot, they did eat, they drank, they bought, they sold, they planted, they builded:

29 But the same day that Lot went out of Sodom, it rained fire and brimstone from heaven, and destroyed *them* all.

30 Even thus shall it be in the day when the Son of Man is revealed.

31 In that day, he which shall be upon the house-top, and his stuff in the house, let him not come down to take it away: and he that is in the field, let him likewise not return back.

32 Remember Lot's wife.

33 Whosoever shall seek to save his life shall lose it; and whosoever shall lose his life shall preserve it.

34 I tell you, in that night there shall be two *men* in one bed; the one shall be taken, and the other shall be left.

35 Two *women* shall be grinding together; the one shall be taken, and the other left.

36 Two *men* shall be in the field; the one shall be taken, and the other left.

L.

CHAP. XVIII.

The importunate widow.

AND he spake a parable unto them, *to this end*, that men ought always *to* pray, and not to faint;

2 Saying, There was in a city a judge, which feared not God, neither regarded man:

3 And there was a widow in that city; and she came unto him, saying, Avenge me of mine adversary.

4 And he would not for a while: but afterward he said within himself, Though I fear not God, nor regard man;

5 Yet, because this widow troubleth me, I will avenge her, lest by her continual coming she weary me.

6 And the Lord said, Hear what the unjust judge saith.

7 And shall not God avenge his own elect, which cry day and night unto him, though he bear long with them?

8 I tell you, that he will avenge them speedily. Nevertheless, when the Son of Man cometh, shall he find faith on the earth?

9 And he spake this parable unto certain which trusted in themselves, that they were righteous, and despised others:

10 Two men went up into the temple to pray; the one a Pharisee, and the other a publican.

11 The Pharisee stood and prayed thus with himself, God, I thank thee, that I am not as other men *are*, extortioners, unjust, adulterers, or even as this publican.

12 I fast twice in the week, I give tithes of all that I possess.

13 And the publican, standing afar off, would not lift up so much as *his* eyes unto heaven, but smote upon his breast, saying, God be merciful to me a sinner.

14 I tell you, this man went down to his house justified *rather* than the other: for every one that exalteth himself shall be abased; and he that humbleth himself shall be exalted.

38 Now it came to pass, as they went, that he entered into a certain village: and a certain woman, named Martha, received him into her house.

39 And she had a sister called Mary, which also sat at Jesus' feet, and heard his word.

40 But Martha was cumbered about much serving, and came to him, and said, Lord, dost thou not care that my sister hath left me to serve alone? bid her, therefore, that she help me.

41 And Jesus, answered, and said unto her, Martha, Martha, thou art careful, and troubled about many things:

42 But one thing is needful: and Mary hath chosen that good part, which shall not be taken away from her.

AND it came to pass, *that*, when Jesus had finished these sayings, he departed from Galilee, and came into the coasts of Judea beyond Jordan:

2 And great multitudes followed him,

3 The Pharisees also came unto him, tempting him, and saying unto him, Is it lawful for a man to put away his wife for every cause?

4 And he answered and said unto them, Have ye not read, that he which made *them* at the beginning, made them male and female?

5 And said, For this cause shall a man leave father and mother, and shall cleave to his wife; and they twain shall be one flesh.

6 Wherefore they are no more twain, but one flesh. What, therefore, God hath joined together, let no man put asunder.

7 They say unto him, Why did Moses then command to give a writing of divorcement, and to put her away?

8 He saith unto them, Moses, because of the hardness of your hearts, suffered you to put away your wives: but from the beginning it was not so.

9 And I say unto you, Whosoever shall put away his wife, except *it be* for fornication, and shall marry another, committeth adultery: and whoso marrieth her which is put away doth commit adultery.

10 His disciples say unto him, If the case of the man be so with *his* wife, it is not good to marry.

11 But he said unto them, All *men* cannot receive this saying, save *they* to whom it is given.

12 For there are some eunuchs, which were so born from *their* of heaven's sake. He that is able to receive *it*, let him receive *it*.

13 Then were there brought unto him little children, that he should put *his* hands on them and pray: and the disciples rebuked them.

14 But Jesus said, Suffer little children, and forbid them not, to come unto me: for of such is the kingdom of heaven.

15 And he laid *his* hands on them, and departed thence.

16 And, behold, one came and said unto him, Good Master, what good thing shall I do, that I may have eternal life?

17 And he said unto him, Why callest thou me good? *there is* none good but one, *that is*, God: but if thou wilt enter into life, keep the commandments.

18 He saith unto him, Which? Jesus said, Thou shalt do no murder, Thou shalt not commit adultery, Thou shalt not steal, Thou shalt not bear false witness,

19 Honour thy father and *thy* mother: and, Thou shalt love thy neighbour as thyself.

20 The young man saith unto him, All these things have I kept from my youth up: what lack I yet?

21 Jesus said unto him, If thou wilt be perfect, go *and* sell that thou hast, and give to the poor, and thou shalt have treasure in heaven: and come *and* follow me.

22 But when the young man heard that saying, he went away sorrowful: for he had great possessions.

23 Then said Jesus unto his disciples, Verily I say unto you, That a rich man shall hardly enter into the kingdom of heaven.

24 And again I say unto you, It is easier for a camel to go through the eye of a needle, than for a rich man to enter into the kingdom of God.

25 When his disciples heard *it*, they were exceedingly amazed, saying, Who then can be saved?

26 But Jesus beheld *them*, and said unto them, With men this is impossible; but with God all things are possible.

CHAP. XX.

The labourers in the vineyard.

FOR the kingdom of heaven is like unto a man *that is* an householder, which went out early in the morning to hire labourers into his vineyard.

2 And when he had agreed with the labourers for a penny a day, he sent them into his vineyard.

3 And he went out about the third hour, and saw others standing idle in the market-place,

4 And said unto them, Go ye also into the vineyard; and whatsoever is right I will give you. And they went their way.

5 Again he went out about the sixth and ninth hour, and did likewise.

6 And about the eleventh hour he went out, and found others standing idle, and saith unto them, Why stand ye here all the day idle?

7 They say unto him, Because no man hath hired us. He saith unto them, Go ye also into the vineyard; and whatsoever is right, *that* shall ye receive.

8 So when even was come, the lord of the vineyard saith unto his steward, Call the labourers, and give them *their* hire, beginning from the last unto the first.

9 And when they came that *were hired* about the eleventh hour, they received every man a penny.

10 But when the first came, they supposed that they should have received more; and they likewise received every man a penny.

11 And when they had received *it*, they murmured against the good man of the house,

12 Saying, These last have wrought *but* one hour, and thou hast made them equal unto us, which have borne the burden and heat of the day.

13 But he answered one of them, and said, Friend, I do thee no wrong: didst not thou agree with me for a penny?

14 Take *that* thine *is*, and go thy way: I will give unto this last, even as unto thee.

15 Is it not lawful for me to do what I will with mine own? is thine eye evil because I am good?

16 So the last shall be first, and the first last: for many be called, but few chosen.

CHAP. XIX.

The publican Zacchæus.

AND *Jesus* entered and passed through Jericho.

2 And, behold, *there was* a man named Zaccheus, which was the chief among the publicans, and he was rich.

3 And he sought to see Jesus who he was; and could not for the press, because he was little of stature.

4 And he ran before, and climbed up into a sycamore-tree to see him; for he was to pass that *way*.

5 And, when Jesus came to the place, he looked up, and saw him, and said unto him, Zaccheus, make haste, and come down; for to-day I must abide at thy house.

6 And he made haste, and came down, and received him joyfully.

7 And when they saw *it*, they all murmured, saying, That he was gone to be guest with a man that is a sinner.

8 And Zaccheus stood, and said unto the Lord, Behold, Lord, the half of my goods I give to the poor; and if I have taken any thing from any man by false accusation, I restore him fourfold.

9 And Jesus said unto him, This day is salvation come to this house, forasmuch as he also is a son of Abraham.

10 For the Son of Man is come to seek and to save that which was lost.

11 And, as they heard these things, he added, and spake a parable, because he was nigh to Jerusalem, and because they thought that the kingdom of God should immediately appear.

12 He said, therefore, A certain nobleman went into a far country to receive for himself a kingdom, and to return.

13 And he called his ten servants, and delivered them ten pounds, and said unto them, Occupy till I come.

14 But his citizens hated him, and sent a message after him, saying, We will not have this *man* to reign over us.

15 And it came to pass, that when he was returned, having received the kingdom, then he commanded these servants to be called unto him, to whom he had given the money, that he might know how much every man had gained by trading.

16 Then came the first, saying, Lord, thy pound hath gained ten pounds.

17 And he said unto him, Well, thou good servant; because thou hast been faithful in a very little, have thou authority over ten cities.

18 And the second came, saying, Lord, thy pound hath gained five pounds.

19 And he said likewise to him, Be thou also over five cities.

20 And another came, saying, Lord, behold, *here is* thy pound, which I have kept laid up in a napkin:

21 For I feared thee, because thou art an austere man; thou takest up that thou layedst not down, and reapest that thou didst not sow.

22 And he saith unto him, Out of thine own mouth will I judge thee, *thou* wicked servant. Thou knewest that I was an austere man, taking up that I laid not down, and reaping that I did not sow:

K2

23 Wherefore then gavest not thou my money into the bank, that at my coming I might have required mine own with usury?

24 And he said unto them that stood by, Take from him the pound, and give *it* to him that hath ten pounds. L. 19.

25 (And they said unto him, Lord, he hath ten pounds.)

26 For I say unto you, That unto every one which hath, shall be given; and from him that hath not, even that he hath, shall be taken away from him.

27 But those mine enemies, which would not that I should reign over them, bring hither, and slay *them* before me.

28 And when he had thus spoken, he went before, ascending up to Jerusalem.

AND when they drew nigh unto Jerusalem, and were come to Bethpage, unto the mount of Olives, then sent Jesus two disciples, M. 21.

2 Saying unto them, Go into the village over against you, and straightway ye shall find an ass tied, and a colt with her: loose *them*, and bring *them* unto me.

3 And if any *man* say aught unto you, ye shall say, The Lord hath need of them; and straightway he will send them.

6 And the disciples went, and did as Jesus commanded them,

7 And brought the ass, and the colt, and put on them their clothes, and they set *him* thereon.

8 And a very great multitude spread their garments in the way; others cut down branches from the trees, and strawed them in the way.

10 And when he was come into Jerusalem, all the city was moved, saying, Who is this?

19 The Pharisees, therefore, said among themselves, Perceive ye how ye prevail nothing? behold, the world is gone after him. J. 12.

20 And there were certain Greeks among them, that came up to worship at the feast:

21 The same came, therefore, to Philip, which was of Bethsaida of Galilee, and desired him, saying, Sir, we would see Jesus. J. 12.

22 Philip cometh and telleth Andrew: and again, Andrew and Philip tell Jesus.

23 And Jesus answered them, saying,

24 Verily, verily, I say unto you, Except a corn of wheat fall into the ground and die, it abideth alone: but if it die, it bringeth forth much fruit.

17 And he left them, and went out of the city into Bethany; and he lodged there. M. 21.

12 And on the morrow, when they were come from Bethany, Mk. 11

15. Jesus went into the temple, and began to cast out them that sold and bought in the temple, and overthrew the tables of the money-changers, and the seats of them that sold doves;

16 And would not suffer that any man should carry *any* v…
through the temple.

17 And he taught, saying …
them, Is it not written, My h…
shall be called of all nations …
house of prayer? but ye …
made it a den of thieves.

18 And the scribes and …
priests heard *it*, and sought …
they might destroy him: for …
feared him, because all the pe…
was astonished at his doctrin…

19 And when even was co…
he went out of the city. +27 Mark 11.2

28 But what think ye? A *certain* man had two sons; and he came to the first, and said, Son, go work to-day in my vineyard. M. 21.

29 He answered and said, I will not: but afterward he repented, and went.

30 And he came to the second, and said likewise. And he answered and said, I *go*, sir: and went not.

31 Whether of them twain did the will of *his* father? They say unto him, The first. Jesus saith unto them, Verily I say unto you, That the publicans and the harlots go into the kingdom of God before you.

33 Hear another parable: A certain M. 21
man planted a vineyard, and set Mk. 12
an hedge about *it*, and digged *a place for* the wine-fat, and built a tower, and let it out to husbandmen, and went into a far country.

2 And at the season he sent to the husbandmen a servant, that he might receive from the husbandmen of the fruit of the vineyard.

3 And they caught *him*, and beat him, and sent *him* away empty.

4 And again he sent unto them another servant; and at him they cast stones, and wounded *him* in the head, and sent *him* away shamefully handled.

5 And again he sent another; and him they killed, and many others; beating some, and killing some.

6 Having yet, therefore, one son, his well-beloved, he sent him also last unto them, saying, They will reverence my son.

7 But those husbandmen said among themselves, This is the heir; come, let us kill him, and the inheritance shall be ours.

8 And they took him, and killed *him*, and cast *him* out of the vineyard.

9 What shall, therefore, the lord of the vineyard do? he will come and destroy the husbandmen, and will give the vineyard unto others.

45 And when the chief priests M. 21
and Pharisees had heard his parables, they perceived that he spake of them.

46 But when they sought to lay hands on him, they feared the multitude, because they took him for a prophet.

AND Jesus answered, and M. 22
spake unto them again by parables, and said,

2 The kingdom of heaven is like unto a certain king, which made a marriage for his son,

3 And sent forth his servants to call them that were bidden to the wedding; and they would not come.

4 Again, he sent forth other servants, saying, Tell them which are M.
bidden, Behold, I have prepared my dinner: my oxen and *my* fatlings *are* killed, and all things *are* ready: come unto the marriage.

5 But they made light of *it*, and went their ways, one to his farm, another to his merchandise:

6 And the remnant took his servants, and intreated *them* spitefully, and slew *them*.

7 But when the king heard *thereof*, he was wroth: and he sent forth his armies, and destroyed those murderers, and burnt up their city.

8 Then saith he to his servants, The wedding is ready, but they which were bidden were not worthy.

9 Go ye therefore into the highways, and, as many as ye shall find, bid to the marriage.

10 So those servants went out into the highways, and gathered together all as many as they found, both bad and good: and the wedding was furnished with guests.

11 And when the king came in to see the guests, he saw there a man which had not on a wedding garment:

12 And he saith unto him, Friend, how camest thou in hither, not having a wedding garment? And he was speechless.

13 Then saith the king to the servants, Bind him hand and foot, and take him away, and cast *him* into outer darkness; there shall be weeping and gnashing of teeth.

14 For many are called, but few *are* chosen.

15 Then went the Pharisees, and took counsel how they might entangle him in *his* talk.

16 And they sent out unto him their disciples, with the Herodians, saying, Master, we know that thou art true, and teachest the way of God in truth, neither carest thou for any *man*: for thou regardest not the person of men.

17 Tell us, therefore, What thinkest thou? Is it lawful to give tribute unto Cesar, or not?

18 But Jesus perceived their

wickedness, and said, Why tempt ye me, ye hypocrites? M. 22
19 Shew me the tribute-money. And they brought unto him a penny.
20 And he saith unto them, Whose *is* this image and superscription?
21 They say unto him, Cesar's. Then saith he unto them, Render, therefore, unto Cesar the things which are Cesar's; and unto God the things that are God's.
22 When they had heard *these words*, they marvelled, and left him, and went their way.
23 The same day came to him the Sadducees, which say that there is no resurrection, and asked him,
24 Saying, Master, Moses said, If a man die, having no children, his brother shall marry his wife, and raise up seed unto his brother.
25 Now, there were with us seven brethren: and the first, when he had married a wife, deceased; and having no issue, left his wife unto his brother:
26 Likewise the second also, and the third, unto the seventh.
27 And last of all the woman died also.
28 Therefore, in the resurrection, whose wife shall she be of the seven? for they all had her.
29 Jesus answered, and said unto them, Ye do err, not knowing the scriptures, nor the power of God.
30 For in the resurrection they neither marry, nor are given in marriage; but are as the angels of God in heaven.
31 But as touching the resurrection of the dead, have ye not read that which was spoken unto you by God, saying,
32 I am the God of Abraham, and the God of Isaac, and the God of Jacob? God is not the God of the dead, but of the living.
33 And when the multitude heard *this*, they were astonished at his doctrine.

28 And one of the scribes came, and having heard them reasoning together, and perceiving that he had answered them well, asked him, Which is the first commandment of all? Mk. 12.
29 And Jesus answered him, The first of all the commandments *is*, Hear, O Israel; The Lord our God is one Lord:
30 And thou shalt love the Lord thy God with all thy heart, and with all thy soul, and with all thy mind, and with all thy strength: This *is* the first commandment.
31 And the second *is* like, *namely* this, Thou shalt love thy neighbour as thyself. There is none other commandment greater than these.
40 On these two commandments hang all the law and the prophets. M. 22
32 And the scribe said unto him, Well, Master, thou hast said the truth: for there is one God; and there is none other but he: Mk. 12.
33 And to love him with all the heart, and with all the understanding, and with all the soul, and with all the strength, and to love *his* neighbour as himself, is more than all whole burnt-offerings and sacrifices.

CHAP. XXIII. M.

The Pharisees exposed, &c.

THEN spake Jesus to the multitude, and to his disciples
2 Saying, The scribes and the Pharisees sit in Moses' seat:
3 All therefore whatsoever they bid you observe, *that* observe and do; but do not ye after their works: for they say and do not.
4 For they bind heavy burdens and grievous to be borne, and lay *them* on mens' shoulders; but they *themselves* will not move them with one of their fingers.
5 But all their works they do for to be seen of men: they make broad their phylacteries, and enlarge the borders of their garments.
6 And love the uppermost rooms at feasts, and the chief seats in the synagogues.

7 And greetings in the markets, and to be called of men, Rabbi, Rabbi.

8 But be not ye called Rabbi; for one is your Master, *even* Christ; and all ye are brethren.

9 And call no *man* your Father upon the earth: for one is your Father, which is in heaven.

10 Neither be ye called masters: for one is your master, *even* Christ.

11 But he that is greatest among you shall be your servant.

12 And whosoever shall exalt himself shall be abased; and he that shall humble himself shall be exalted.

13 But woe unto you, scribes and Pharisees, hypocrites! for ye shut up the kingdom of heaven against men: for ye neither go in *yourselves*, neither suffer ye them that are entering, to go in.

14 Woe unto you, scribes and Pharisees, hypocrites! for ye devour widows' houses, and for a pretence make long prayer: therefore ye shall receive the greater damnation.

15 Woe unto you, scribes and Pharisees, hypocrites! for ye compass sea and land to make one proselyte; and when he is made, ye make him two-fold more the child of hell than yourselves.

16 Woe unto you, *ye* blind guides! which say, Whosoever shall swear by the temple, it is nothing; but whosoever shall swear by the gold of the temple, he is a debtor.

17 *Ye* fools and blind! for whether *is* greater, the gold, or the temple that sanctifieth the gold?

18 And, whosoever shall swear by the altar, it is nothing; but whosoever sweareth by the gift that is upon it, he is guilty.

19 *Ye* fools, and blind! for whether *is* greater, the gift, or the altar that sanctifieth the gift?

20 Whoso, therefore, shall swear by the altar, sweareth by it, and by all things thereon.

21 And whoso shall swear by the temple, sweareth by it, and by him that dwelleth therein.

22 And he that shall swear by heaven, sweareth by the throne of God, and by him that sitteth thereon.

23 Woe unto you, scribes and Pharisees, hypocrites! for ye pay tithe of mint, and anise, and cummin, and have omitted the weightier *matters* of the law, judgment, mercy, and faith: these ought ye to have done, and not to leave the other undone.

24 *Ye* blind guides! which strain at a gnat, and swallow a camel.

25 Woe unto you, scribes and Pharisees, hypocrites! for ye make clean the outside of the cup and of the platter, but within they are full of extortion and excess.

26 *Thou* blind Pharisee, cleanse first that *which* is within the cup and platter, that the outside of them may be clean also.

27 Woe unto you, scribes and Pharisees, hypocrites! for ye are like unto whited sepulchres, which indeed appear beautiful outward, but are within full of dead *mens'* bones, and of all uncleanness.

28 Even so ye also outwardly appear righteous unto men, but within ye are full of hypocrisy and iniquity.

29 Woe unto you, scribes and Pharisees, hypocrites! because ye build the tombs of the prophets, and garnish the sepulchres of the righteous,

30 And say, If we had been in the days of our fathers, we would not have been partakers with them in the blood of the prophets.

31 Wherefore ye be witnesses unto yourselves, that ye are the children of them which killed the prophets.

32 Fill ye up then the measure of your fathers.

33 *Ye* serpents, *ye* generation of vipers! how can ye escape the damnation of hell?

Mk. 12

41 And Jesus sat over against the treasury, and beheld how the people cast money into the treasury; and many that were rich cast in much.

42 And there came a certain poor widow, and she threw in two mites, which make a farthing.

43 And he called *unto him* his disciples, and saith unto them, Verily I say unto you, That this poor widow hath cast more in than all they which have cast into the treasury:

44 For all *they* did cast in of their abundance; but she of her want did cast in all that she had, *even* all her living.

M.

CHAP. XXIV.

Jerusalem's destruction foretold.

AND Jesus went out, and departed from the temple; and his disciples came *to him*, for to shew him the buildings of the temple.

2 And Jesus said unto them, See ye not all these things? Verily I say unto you, There shall not be left here one stone upon another, that shall not be thrown down.

16 Then let them which be in Judea flee into the mountains:

17 Let him which is on the house-top not come down to take any thing out of his house:

18 Neither let him which is in the field return back to take his clothes

19 And woe unto them that are with child, and to them that give suck in those days!

20 But pray ye that your flight be not in the winter, neither on the sabbath-day:

21 For then shall be great tribulation, such as was not since the beginning of the world to this time, no, nor ever shall be.

29 Immediately after the tribulation of those days shall the sun be darkened, and the moon shall not give her light, and the stars shall fall from heaven, and the powers of the heavens shall be shaken:

M. 24

32 Now learn a parable of the fig-tree; When his branch is yet tender, and putteth forth leaves, ye know that summer *is* nigh:

33 So likewise ye, when ye shall see all these things, know that it is near, *even* at the doors.

36 But of that day and hour knoweth no *man*; no, not the angels of heaven, but my Father only.

37 But as the days of Noe *were*, so shall also the coming of the Son of Man be.

38 For as in the days that were before the flood they were eating and drinking, marrying and giving in marriage, until the day that Noe entered into the ark,

39 And knew not until the flood came, and took them all away;

40 Then shall two be in the field; the one shall be taken, and the other left.

41 Two *women shall be* grinding at the mill; the one shall be taken, and the other left.

42 Watch, therefore; for ye know not what hour your Lord doth come.

43 But know this, that if the good man of the house had known in what watch the thief would come, he would have watched, and would not have suffered his house to be broken up.

44 Therefore be ye also ready:

45 Who then is a faithful and wise servant, whom his lord hath made ruler over his household, to give them meat in due season?

46 Blessed *is* that servant, whom his lord, when he cometh, shall find so doing.

47 Verily I say unto you, That he shall make him ruler over all his goods.

48 But and if that evil servant shall say in his heart, My lord delayeth his coming;

49 And shall begin to smite *his* fellow-servants, and to eat and drink with the drunken;

50 The lord of that servant shal come in a day when he looket not for *him*, and in an hour tha he is not aware of.

51 And shall cut him asunde and appoint *him* his portion wit the hypocrites: there shall b weeping and gnashing of teeth.

CHAP. XXV.

Parable of the ten virgins.

THEN shall the kingdom of heaven be likened unto ten virgins, which took their lamps, and went forth to meet the bridegroom.

2 And five of them were wise, and five *were* foolish.

3 They that *were* foolish took their lamps, and took no oil with them:

4 But the wise took oil in their vessels with their lamps.

5 While the bridegroom tarried, they all slumbered and slept.

6 And at midnight there was a cry made, Behold, the bridegroom cometh; go ye out to meet him.

7 Then all those virgins arose, and trimmed their lamps.

8 And the foolish said unto the wise, Give us of your oil; for our lamps are gone out.

9 But the wise answered, saying, *Not so*: lest there be not enough for us and you: but go ye rather to them that sell, and buy for yourselves.

10 And while they went to buy, the bridegroom came; and they that were ready went in with him to the marriage: and the door was shut.

11 Afterward came also the other virgins, saying, Lord, Lord, open to us.

12 But he answered and said, Verily I say unto you, I know you not.

13 Watch, therefore

14 For *the kingdom of heaven is* as a man travelling into a far country, *who* called his own servants, and delivered unto them his goods.

15 And unto one he gave five talents, to another two, and to another one; to every man according to his several ability; and straightway took his journey.

16 Then he that had received the five talents went and traded with the same, and made *them* other five talents.

17 And likewise he that *had received* two, he also gained other two.

18 But he that had received one, went and digged in the earth, and hid his lord's money.

19 After a long time the lord of those servants cometh, and reckoneth with them.

20 And so he that had received five talents came, and brought other five talents, saying, Lord, thou deliveredst unto me five talents: behold, I have gained beside them five talents more.

21 His lord said unto him, Well done, *thou* good and faithful servant: thou hast been faithful over a few things, I will make thee ruler over many things: enter thou into the joy of thy lord.

22 He also that had received two talents came, and said, Lord, thou deliveredst unto me two talents: behold, I have gained two other talents beside them.

23 His lord said unto him, Well done, good and faithful servant: thou hast been faithful over a few things, I will make thee ruler over many things: enter thou into the joy of thy lord.

24 Then he which had received the one talent came, and said, Lord, I knew thee, that thou art an hard man, reaping where thou hast not sown, and gathering where thou hast not strawed:

25 And I was afraid, and went and hid thy talent in the earth: lo, *there* thou hast *that is* thine.

26 His lord answered, and said unto him, *Thou* wicked and slothful servant, thou knewest that I reap where I sowed not, and gather where I have not strawed:

M. 25

27 Thou oughtest, therefore, to have put my money to the exchangers, and *then* at my coming I should have received mine own with usury.

28 Take, therefore, the talent from him, and give it unto him which hath ten talents.

29 For unto every one that hath shall be given, and he shall have abundance: but from him that hath not, shall be taken away even that which he hath.

30 And cast ye the unprofitable servant into outer darkness: there shall be weeping and gnashing of teeth.

L. 21

34 And take heed to yourselves, lest at any time your hearts be overcharged with surfeiting, and drunkenness, and cares of this life, and *so* that day come upon you unawares.

35 For as a snare shall it come on all them that dwell on the face of the whole earth.

36 Watch ye, therefore, and pray always, that ye may be accounted worthy to escape all these things that shall come to pass, and to stand before the Son of Man.

M. 25

31 When the Son of Man shall come in his glory, and all the holy angels with him, then shall he sit upon the throne of his glory:

32 And before him shall be gathered all nations: and he shall separate them one from another, as a shepherd divideth his sheep from the goats:

33 And he shall set the sheep on his right hand, but the goats on the left.

34 Then shall the King say unto them on his right hand, Come, ye blessed of my Father, inherit the kingdom prepared for you from the foundation of the world:

35 For I was an hungered, and ye gave me meat: I was thirsty, and ye gave me drink: I was a stranger, and ye took me in:

36 Naked, and ye clothed me: I was sick, and ye visited me: I was in prison, and ye came unto me.

M. 25

37 Then shall the righteous answer him, saying, Lord, when saw we thee an hungered, and fed *thee?* or thirsty, and gave *thee* drink?

38 When saw we thee a stranger, and took *thee* in? or naked, and clothed *thee?*

39 Or when saw we thee sick, or in prison, and came unto *thee?*

40 And the King shall answer, and say unto them, Verily I say unto you, Inasmuch as ye have done *it* unto one of the least of these my brethren, ye have done *it* unto me.

41 Then shall he say also unto them on the left hand, Depart from me, ye cursed, into everlasting fire, prepared for the devil and his angels:

42 For I was an hungered, and ye gave me no meat: I was thirsty, and ye gave me no drink:

43 I was a stranger, and ye took me not in: naked, and ye clothed me not: sick, and in prison, and ye visited me not.

44 Then shall they also answer him, saying, Lord, when saw we *thee* an hungered, or athirst, or a stranger, or naked, or sick, or in prison, and did not minister unto thee?

45 Then shall he answer them, saying, Verily I say unto you, Inasmuch as ye did *it* not to one of the least of these, ye did *it* not to me.

46 And these shall go away into everlasting punishment: but the righteous into life eternal.

Mk. 14

CHAP. XIV.

Conspiracy against Christ.

AFTER two days was *the feast* of the passover, and of unleavened bread: and the chief priests and the scribes sought how they might take him by craft, and put *him* to death.

2 But they said, Not on the feast-*day*, lest there be an uproar of the people.

3 And being in Bethany, in the house of Simon the leper, as he sat at meat, there came a woman

Mk.14

having an alabaster-box of oint-
ment of spikenard, very precious:
and she brake the box, and pour-
ed *it* on his head.
4 And there were some that had
indignation within themselves,
and said, Why was this waste of
the ointment made?
5 For it might have been sold for
more than three hundred pence,
and have been given to the poor.
And they murmured against her.
6 And Jesus said, Let her alone,
why trouble ye her? she hath
wrought a good work on me.
7 For ye have the poor with you
always, and whensoever ye will,
ye may do them good; but me ye
have not always.
8 She hath done what she could;
she is come aforehand to anoint
my body to the burying.

M.26

14 Then one of the twelve call-
ed Judas Iscariot, went unto the
chief priests,
15 And said *unto them*, What will
ye give me, and I will deliver him
unto you? And they covenanted
with him for thirty pieces of silver.
16 And from that time he sought
opportunity to betray him.
17 Now, the first *day* of the *feast*
of unleavened bread, the disciples
came to Jesus, saying unto him,
Where wilt thou that we prepare
for thee to eat the passover?
18 And he said, Go into the city
to such a man, and say unto him,
The Master saith, My time is at
hand; I will keep the passover at
thy house with my disciples.
19 And the disciples did as Je-
sus had appointed them; and
they made ready the passover.
20 Now, when the even was come,
he sat down with the twelve.

L.22

24 And there was also a strife
among them, which of them
should be accounted the greatest.
25 And he said unto them, The
kings of the Gentiles exercise
lordship over them; and they that
exercise authority upon them are
called benefactors.

L.2

26 But ye *shall* not *be* so: but he
that is greatest among you, let
him be as the younger; and he
that is chief, as he that doth serve.
27 For whether *is* greater, he
that sitteth at meat, or he that
serveth? *is* not he that sitteth at
meat? but I am among you as he
that serveth.

J.13

2 And supper being ended,
4 He riseth from supper, and laid
aside his garments; and took a
towel, and girded himself.
5 After that he poureth water in-
to a bason, and began to wash the
disciples' feet, and to wipe them
with the towel wherewith he was
girded.
6 Then cometh he to Simon Pe-
ter: and Peter saith unto him,
Lord, dost thou wash my feet?
7 Jesus answered, and said unto
him, What I do, thou knowest not
now; but thou shalt know hereafter.
8 Peter saith unto him, Thou
shalt never wash my feet. Jesus
answered him, If I wash thee not,
thou hast no part with me.
9 Simon Peter saith unto him,
Lord, not my feet only, but also
my hands and *my* head.
10 Jesus saith to him, He that
is washed, needeth not, save to
wash *his* feet, but is clean every
whit: and ye are clean, but not all.
11 For he knew who should be-
tray him; therefore said he, Ye
are not all clean.
12 So, after he had washed their
feet, and had taken his garments,
and was set down again, he said
unto them, Know ye what I have
done to you?
13 Ye call me Master and Lord:
and ye say well; for *so* I am.
14 If I then, *your* Lord and Mas-
ter, have washed your feet, ye also
ought to wash one another's feet.
15 For I have given you an ex-
ample, that ye should do as I have
done to you.
16 Verily, verily, I say unto you,
The servant is not greater than
his lord: neither he that is sent,
greater than he that sent him.
17 If ye know these things, hap-
py are ye if ye do them.

21 When Jesus had thus said, he J. 13.
was troubled in spirit, and testified, and said, Verily, verily, I say unto you, that one of you shall betray me.

22 Then the disciples looked one on another, doubting of whom he spake.

23 Now there was leaning on Jesus' bosom one of his disciples, whom Jesus loved.

24 Simon Peter, therefore, beckoned to him, that he should ask who it should be of whom he spake.

25 He then, lying on Jesus' breast, saith unto him, Lord, who is it?

26 Jesus answered, He it is, to whom I shall give a sop, when I have dipped *it*. And when he had dipped the sop, he gave *it* to Judas Iscariot, *the son* of Simon.

31 Therefore, when he was gone out, Jesus said,

34 A new commandment I give unto you, That ye love one another; as I have loved you, that ye also love one another.

35 By this shall all *men* know that ye are my disciples, if ye have love one to another.

31 Then saith Jesus unto them, M. 26
All ye shall be offended because of me this night:

33 Peter answered, and said unto him, Though all *men* shall be offended because of thee, *yet* will I never be offended.

33 I am ready to go with thee, both L. 22
into prison, and to death.

34 And he said, I tell thee, Peter, the cock shall not crow this day, before that thou shalt thrice deny that thou knowest me.

M. 26
35 Peter said unto him, Though I should die with thee, yet will I not deny thee. Likewise also said all the disciples.

36 Then cometh Jesus with them unto a place called Gethsemane, and saith unto the disciples, Sit ye here, while I go and pray yonder.

37 And he took with him Peter M. 26.
and the two sons of Zebedee, and began to be sorrowful and very heavy.

38 Then saith he unto them, My soul is exceeding sorrowful, even unto death: tarry ye here, and watch with me.

39 And he went a little farther, and fell on his face, and prayed, saying, O my Father, if it be possible, let this cup pass from me: nevertheless, not as I will, but as thou *wilt*.

40 And he cometh unto the disciples, and findeth them asleep, and saith unto Peter, What! could ye not watch with me one hour?

41 Watch and pray, that ye enter not into temptation: the spirit indeed *is* willing, but the flesh *is* weak.

42 He went away again the second time, and prayed, saying, O my Father, if this cup may not pass away from me, except I drink it, thy will be done.

43 And he came and found them asleep again: for their eyes were heavy.

44 And he left them, and went away again, and prayed the third time, saying the same words.

45 Then cometh he to his disciples, and saith unto them, Sleep on now, and take *your* rest:

J.

CHAP. XVIII.

Judas betrayeth Jesus.

WHEN Jesus had spoken these words, he went forth with his disciples over the brook Cedron, where was a garden, into the which he entered, and his disciples.

2 And Judas also, which betrayed him, knew the place: for Jesus oft-times resorted thither with his disciples.

3 Judas then, having received a band *of men* and officers from the chief priests and Pharisees, cometh thither with lanterns, and torches, and weapons.

M. 26

48 Now he that betrayed him gave them a sign, saying, Whomsoever I shall kiss, that same is he: hold him fast.

49 And forthwith he came to Jesus, and said, Hail, Master, and kissed him.

50 And Jesus said unto him, Friend, wherefore art thou come?

J. 18

4 Jesus, therefore, knowing all things that should come upon him, went forth, and said unto them, Whom seek ye?

5 They answered him, Jesus of Nazareth. Jesus saith unto them, I am *he*. (And Judas also, which betrayed him, stood with them.)

6 As soon then as he had said unto them, I am *he*, they went backward, and fell to the ground.

7 Then asked he them again, Whom seek ye? And they said, Jesus of Nazareth.

8 Jesus answered, I have told you, that I am *he*: if, therefore, ye seek me, let these go their way;

M. 26

50 Then came they and laid hands on Jesus, and took him.

51 And, behold, one of them, which were with Jesus, stretched out *his* hand, and drew his sword, and struck a servant of the high priest, and smote off his ear.

52 Then said Jesus unto him, Put up again thy sword into his place: for all they that take the sword shall perish with the sword.

55 In that same hour said Jesus to the multitudes, Are ye come out as against a thief, with swords, and staves for to take me? I sat daily with you teaching in the temple, and ye laid no hold on me.

56. Then all the disciples forsook him and fled.

Mk. 14

51 And there followed him a certain young man, having a linen cloth cast about *his* naked *body*; and the young men laid hold on him:

52 And he left the linen cloth, and fled from them naked.

M. 2

57 And they that had laid hold on Jesus, led *him* away to Caiaphas the high priest, where the scribes and the elders were assembled.

J. 1

15 And Simon Peter followed Jesus, and *so did* another disciple. That disciple was known unto the high priest, and went in with Jesus into the palace of the high priest.

16 But Peter stood at the door without. Then went out that other disciple, which was known unto the high priest, and spake unto her that kept the door, and brought in Peter.

18 And the servants and officers stood there, who had made a fire of coals, (for it was cold,) and they warmed themselves: and Peter stood with them, and warmed himself.

17 Then saith the damsel, that kept the door, unto Peter, Art not thou also *one* of this man's disciples? He saith, I am not.

25 And Simon Peter stood and warmed himself: they said, therefore, unto him, Art not thou also *one* of his disciples? He denied *it*, and said, I am not.

26 One of the servants of the high priest, (being *his* kinsman whose ear Peter cut off,) saith, Did not I see thee in the garden with him?

27 Peter then denied again; and immediately the cock crew.

M. 2

75 And Peter remembered the words of Jesus, which said unto him, Before the cock crow, thou shalt deny me thrice. And he went out, and wept bitterly.

J. 1

19 The high priest then asked Jesus of his disciples, and of his doctrine.

20 Jesus answered him, I spake openly to the world; I ever taught in the synagogue, and in the temple, whither the Jews always resort; and in secret have I said nothing.

21 Why askest thou me? ask J. 18.
them which heard me, what I
have said unto them: behold, they
know what I said.
22 And, when he had thus spoken,
one of the officers which stood by
struck Jesus with the palm of his
hand, saying, Answerest thou the
high priest so?
23 Jesus answered him, If I have
spoken evil, bear witness of the evil;
but if well, why smitest thou me?
53 And they led Jesus away to Mk. 14
the high priest; and with him were
assembled all the chief priests,
and the elders, and the scribes.
55 And the chief priests, and all
the council sought for witness
against Jesus to put him to death;
and found none:
56 For many bare false witness
against him, but their witness
agreed not together.
57 And there arose certain, and
bare false witness against him,
saying,
58 We heard him say, I will destroy
this temple that is made with
hands, and within three days I will
build another made without hands.
59 But neither so did their witness
agree together.
60 And the high priest stood up
in the midst, and asked Jesus, saying,
Answerest thou nothing? what
is it which these witness against
thee.
61 But he held his peace, and answered
nothing. Again the high
priest asked him, and said unto
him, Art thou the Christ, the Son
of the Blessed?
67 And he said unto them, If L. 22.
I tell you, ye will not believe:
68 And if I also ask *you*, ye will
not answer me, nor let *me* go.
70 Then said they all, Art thou
then the Son of God? And he
said unto them, Ye say that I am.
63 Then the high priest rent his Mk. 14.
clothes, and saith, What need we
any further witnesses?
64 Ye have heard the blasphemy:
what think ye? And they
all condemned him to be guilty of Mk. 14.
death.
65 And some began to spit on
him, and to cover his face, and to
buffet him, and to say unto him,
Prophesy: and the servants did
strike him with the palms of their
hands, J. 18. 28
28 Then led they Jesus from Caiaphas unto the hall of judgment,
and it was early; and they
themselves went not into the judgment-hall,
lest they should be defiled;
but that they might eat the
passover.
29 Pilate then went out unto
them, and said, What accusation
bring ye against this man?
30 They answered, and said unto
him, If he were not a malefactor,
we would not have delivered
him up unto thee.
31 Then said Pilate unto them,
Take ye him, and judge him according
to your law. The Jews,
therefore, said unto him, It is not
lawful for us to put any man to
death;
33 Then Pilate entered into the
judgment-hall again, and called
Jesus, and said unto him, Art
thou the King of the Jews?
34 Jesus answered him, Sayest
thou this thing of thyself, or did
others tell it thee of me?
35 Pilate answered, Am I a Jew?
Thine own nation and the chief
priests have delivered thee unto
me. What hast thou done?
36 Jesus answered, My kingdom
is not of this world. If my kingdom
were of this world, then would
my servants fight, that I should not
be delivered to the Jews: but now
is my kingdom not from hence.
37 Pilate, therefore, said unto him,
Art thou a King then? Jesus answered,
thou sayest that I am a
king. To this end was I born,
and for this cause came I into the
world, that I should bear witness
unto the truth. Every one that is
of the truth heareth my voice.
38 Pilate saith unto him, What
is truth? And when he had said
this, he went out again unto the
Jews, and saith unto them, I find
in him no fault *at all*.

L. 23

5 And they were the more fierce, saying, He stirreth up the people, teaching throughout all Jewry, beginning from Galilee to this place.

M. 27

13 Then said Pilate unto him, Hearest thou not how many things they witness against thee?

L. 23

6 When Pilate heard of Galilee, he asked whether the man were a Galilean.

7 And as soon as he knew that he belonged unto Herod's jurisdiction, he sent him to Herod, who himself also was at Jerusalem at that time.

8 And when Herod saw Jesus, he was exceeding glad: for he was desirous to see him of a long *season*, because he had heard many things of him; and he hoped to have seen some miracle done by him.

9 Then he questioned with him in many words; but he answered him nothing.

10 And the chief priests and scribes stood, and vehemently accused him.

11 And Herod, with his men of war, set him at nought, and mocked *him*, and arrayed him in a gorgeous robe, and sent him again to Pilate.

12 And the same day Pilate and Herod were made friends together: for before they were at enmity between themselves.

13 And Pilate, when he had called together the chief priests, and the rulers, and the people,

14 Said unto them, Ye have brought this man unto me, as one* that perverteth the people: and, behold, I, having examined *him* before you, have found no fault in this man, touching those things whereof ye accuse him:

15 No, nor yet Herod: for I sent you to him; and, lo, nothing worthy of death is done unto him:

16 I will, therefore, chastise him, and release *him*.

*under the Roman law de seditiosis in crucem tollendis. Digest de poenis L. 48, tit. 19. l. 28. §3. 'capite plectendi cum saepius seditiose et turbulente se gesserint, et aliquoties adprehensi clementius in eadem temeritate propositi perseveraverint.'

M. 27

15 Now at *that* feast the governor was wont to release unto the people a prisoner, whom they would.

16 And they had then a notable prisoner, called Barabbas.

17 Therefore, when they were gathered together, Pilate said unto them, Whom will ye that I release unto you? Barabbas, or Jesus, which is called Christ?

18 For he knew that for envy they had delivered him.

19 When he was set down on the judgment-seat, his wife sent unto him, saying, Have thou nothing to do with that just man: for I have suffered many things this day in a dream because of him.

20 But the chief priests and elders persuaded the multitude that they should ask Barabbas, and destroy Jesus.

21 The governor answered, and said unto them, Whether of the twain will ye that I release unto you? They said, Barabbas.

22 Pilate saith unto them, What shall I do then with Jesus, which is called Christ? *They* all say unto him, Let him be crucified.

23 And the governor said, Why, what evil hath he done? But they cried out the more, saying, Let him be crucified.

26 Then released he Barabbas unto them; and when he had scourged Jesus, he delivered *him* to be crucified.

27 Then the soldiers of the governor took Jesus into the common hall, and gathered unto him the whole band *of soldiers*.

29 And when they had platted a crown of thorns, they put *it* upon his head, and a reed in his right hand; and they bowed the knee before him, and mocked him, saying, Hail, king of the Jews!

30 And they spit upon him, and took the reed, and smote him on the head.

31 And after that they had mocked him, they took the robe off from him, and put his own raiment on him, and led him away to crucify *him*.

3 Then Judas which had betrayed him, when he saw that he was condemned, repented himself, and brought again the thirty pieces of silver to the chief priests and elders, M. 27.

4 Saying, I have sinned, in that I have betrayed the innocent blood. And they said, What *is that* to us? see thou *to that*.

5 And he cast down the pieces of silver in the temple, and departed, and went and hanged himself.

6 And the chief priests took the silver pieces, and said, It is not lawful for to put them into the treasury, because it is the price of blood.

7 And they took counsel, and bought with them the potter's field, to bury strangers in.

8 Wherefore that field was called, The field of blood, unto this day.

26 And, as they led him away, they laid hold upon one Simon, a Cyrenian, coming out of the country, and on him they laid the cross, that he might bear *it* after Jesus. L. 23

27 And there followed him a great company of people, and of women, which also bewailed and lamented him.

28 But Jesus, turning unto them, said, Daughters of Jerusalem, weep not for me, but weep for yourselves, and for your children.

29 For, behold, the days are coming, in the which they shall say, Blessed *are* the barren, and the wombs that never bare, and the paps which never gave suck.

30 Then shall they begin to say to the mountains, Fall on us; and to the hills, Cover us.

31 For if they do these things in a green tree, what shall be done in the dry?

32 And there were also two others, malefactors, led with him to be put to death.

17 And he, bearing his cross, went forth into a place called *the place* of a skull, which is called in the Hebrew, Golgotha; J. 19

18 Where they crucified him, and two others with him, on either side one, and Jesus in the midst.

19 And Pilate wrote a title, and put it on the cross. And the writing was, JESUS OF NAZARETH, THE KING OF THE JEWS.

20 This title then read many of the Jews: for the place where Jesus was crucified was nigh to the city: and it was written in Hebrew, *and* Greek, *and* Latin.

21 Then said the chief priests of the Jews to Pilate, Write not, The King of the Jews; but that he said, I am King of the Jews.

22 Pilate answered, What I have written, I have written.

23 Then the soldiers, when they had crucified Jesus, took his garments, and made four parts, to every soldier a part, and also *his* coat: now the coat was without seam, woven from the top throughout.

24 They said, therefore, among themselves, Let us not rend it, but cast lots for it, whose it shall be:

39 And they that passed by reviled him, wagging their heads, M. 27.

40 And saying, Thou that destroyest the temple, and buildest *it* in three days, save thyself. If thou be the Son of God, come down from the cross.

41 Likewise also the chief priests mocking *him*, with the scribes and elders, said,

42 He saved others; himself he cannot save. If he be the King of Israel, let him now come down from the cross, and we will believe him.

43 He trusted in God; let him deliver him now, if he will have him: for he said, I am the Son of God.

39 And one of the malefactors, L. 23.
which were hanged, railed on him,
saying, If thou be Christ, save thy-
self and us.
40 But the other, answering, re-
buked him, saying, Dost not thou
fear God, seeing thou art in the
same condemnation?
41 And we indeed justly; for
we receive the due reward of our
deeds: but this man hath done
nothing amiss.
34 Then said Jesus, Father, for-
give them; for they know not
what they do.
25 Now there stood by the cross J. 19
of Jesus, his mother, and his mo-
ther's sister, Mary the *wife* of Cle-
ophas, and Mary Magdalene.
26 When Jesus, therefore, saw
his mother, and the disciple stand-
ing by whom he loved, he saith
unto his mother, Woman, behold
thy Son!
27 Then saith he to the disciple,
Behold thy mother! And from
that hour that disciple took her
unto his own *home*.
46 And about the ninth hour, M. 27
Jesus cried with a loud voice, say-
ing, Eli, Eli, lama sabachthani?
that is to say, My God, my God,
why hast thou forsaken me?
47 Some of them that stood
there, when they heard *that*, said,
This *man* calleth for Elias.
48 And straightway one of them
ran, and took a spunge, and filled
it with vinegar, and put *it* on a
reed, and gave him to drink.
49 The rest said, Let be, let us
see whether Elias will come to
save him.
50 Jesus, when he had cried
again with a loud voice, yielded
up the ghost.
55 And many women were there,
beholding afar off, which follow-
ed Jesus from Galilee, minister-
ing unto him:
56 Among which was Mary
Magdalene, and Mary the mother
of James and Joses, and the mo-
ther of Zebedee's children.

31 The Jews, therefore, because 87
it was the preparation, that the
bodies should not remain upon
the cross on the sabbath-day, (for
that sabbath-day was an high day,)
besought Pilate that their legs
might be broken, and *that* they
might be taken away.
32 Then came the soldiers, and
brake the legs of the first, and of the
other which was crucified with him.
33 But when they came to Je-
sus, and saw that he was dead
already, they brake not his legs:
34 But one of the soldiers with
a spear pierced his side, and
forthwith came thereout blood
and water.
38 And after this, Joseph of Ari-
mathea, (being a disciple of Jesus,
but secretly for fear of the Jews,)
besought Pilate that he might take
away the body of Jesus: and Pilate
gave *him* leave. He came there-
fore, and took the body of Jesus.
39 And there came also Nicode-
mus, (which at the first came to
Jesus by night, and brought a mix-
ture of myrrh and aloes, about an
hundred pound *weight*.
40 Then took they the body of
Jesus, and wound it in linen
clothes with the spices, as the
manner of the Jews is to bury.
41 Now, in the place where he
was crucified, there was a gar-
den; and in the garden a new se-
pulchre, wherein was never man
yet laid.
42 There laid they Jesus,
60. and [redacted] rolled a great M.
stone to the door of the sepul-
chre, and departed.

A New Declaration of Independence for Today's Americans

by
Erik Holden

The basic problem of the human species is group domination of individuals to such an extent that individuals cease to function as such. They become mere functional parts of some group.

This foremost human problem today was already the foremost human problem in the first social organizations known to history. The opposition of short-sighted humans to nature was already showing a tendency to destroy the human species. The continued transfer of individual functions to group functions brings on biological regression. The precedents for biological regression are plentiful; the significance of the evidence is unmistakable.

Biological regression is the long range effect. I will talk about that later. The immediate problem, which leads up to the other, is the misuse of language to manipulate groups. Language becomes dogma for group-control when the words are accepted as coming from an "authority." This is the problem as it has existed throughout all human history.

The problem is not there because it is inherent in the elaborate language humans have developed. It is there because unscrupulous manipulators deliberately put it there — and keep it there. They want to manipulate groups. They have such a limited view of the universe, such a limited view of life and life's meaning, that a petty, short-term group manipulation gives their dwarfed souls and inflated egos some perverted satisfaction.

Two thousand years ago, Jesus identified this problem. He said that it would surely destroy the human species if not corrected. All his teachings, including the profound statement he made by allowing himself to be crucified, pointed out the solution to the problem. Those teachings — and the meaning of his crucifixion — have been twisted backwards.

The story of Jesus has much more significance than many "Christians" give it. Its full significance can only be seen when Jesus is contrasted to the thing he opposed. The thing he opposed was not violence. Violence, per se, is a word without substance. Jesus dealt in realities. Let us look at the realities.

Charges were made against him and he was brought before the official administering the lawful government of the area. The Roman governor found him innocent of any offense against existing laws. What's more, the Roman governor liked Jesus. At the time of the questioning, Pontius Pilate told Jesus, "Almost you persuade me to become a Christian." But a fanatical mob demanded that Jesus be crucified. The individual to individual understanding betwen the governor and Jesus did not hold up under pressure from the mob.

Why? The Roman governor had an organized army that could overpower the mob. Why did he not use it? Why did he make a decision that was neither in keeping with the law, nor in keeping with his own personal judgment?

Pontius Pilate was choosing between two courses of action. On one side was both the law he was supposed to follow and his own personal approval of Jesus. On the other was his knowledge that mobs were the source of his power. He was governor. Control of mobs and *use of mob power* is the basic purpose of every top "authoritarian" official — whether elected or appointed. Pontius Pilate was governor of the area. Against his own perception, he ruled in favor of the mob.

All teachings of Jesus were a condemnation of such a system. He was caught between the Roman and the Jewish systems. He had a good view of both. He was in an area where all individuals were being ground between the two. The broken remnants of past systems served as grist for the grinding. He looked at the whole conglomerate with clear eyes. At his trial he knew what to expect. He faced the verdict calmly. Long before the confrontation he had decided what he would do and what would happen.

Jesus chose the confrontation and crucifixion as the most forceful statement he could make. That statement has never been made more eloquently. Nothing could have pointed up the problem more effectively than that spit-upon figure nailed to the cross — for no reason except that a fanatical mob had demanded it.

The unreasoning mob was the problem. The significance of Jesus hanging on the cross is totally destroyed unless the impulse behind such a mob is examined.

Today a similar mob still exists. Today's mob contains the same elements. The elements are now diluted; the present mob is less homogenous. The significant elements are less conspicuous. The mob is less fanatically committed to a single-minded purpose. But the direction is still the same.

The current mob is the one that most vitally concerns us. It is the one we face this minute. It is, also, far bigger and far more powerful. But the present mob is so confused that extracting the significant mob elements is difficult. *A distorted story of Jesus has become part of the confusion.*

Images of the crucified figure are seen in churches throughout the land. They are called objects of worship. But a perceptive worship of Jesus — as one who gave his life in trying to save the human species from doom — those images are not. Those millions of images are the cruelist nails that still fasten Jesus to the cross.

Officially — by their published dogmas — many "Christian" churches are continuing the crucifixion of Jesus. Certainly, at the very forefront of the mob that is still performing the crucifixion are many who call themselves "Christians." Every time they mouth words praising Jesus for what he was not, they, themselves, are a continuation of the original mob. They are still driving the nails.

They have been driving those nails, that mutilate the teachings of Jesus, for two thousand years. The harm is still done, and the hurt no less, because they are mere unthinking instruments of behind-the-scenes wills, which they do not recognize. The harm is still done, the hurt no less, *and the problem no nearer to solution* because they think Jesus might look down upon them with compassion and say, "Father, forgive them; they know not what they do."

During the short period of time that he lived on earth, Jesus upbraided those who had eyes to see and saw not, ears to hear and heard not — those who listened only to "authoritative" words from officials, those who concentrated their attention on the law and the prophets — those who did not trust their own perception. He taught that individuals could safely transgress against anything, including what people *called* god — but if they transgressed against the holy spirit within themselves they would be doomed beyond redemption.

Note that the entity *Jesus* called god does not manufacture people and give word-laws for their guidance. The god of Jesus does not *create* by waving a wand, like a magician in a circus side show. Jesus taught that the *real* god is more accurately viewed as a father — and people should be viewed as children of that father. He taught that the holy spirit *within each individual* is the individual's basic guide, because everything living has a god *heritage.*

Those who form and manipulate dogma-controlled mobs are the human problem which, as an individual, Jesus opposed.

Let us look first at the age-old human problem, as it existed at the time of Jesus. The detachment of distance may enable us to ignore distracting details and focus only on the significant. Then we can better view the same problem in the confused world that presses in on us today.

Two thousand years ago "serpent" was the word in general use for what is now called a "totalitarian state." It was the word used for a nation controlled by dogmatic, "authoritative" laws that overruled individual perception and individual will. Jesus made it clear that the salvation of the human species depends upon rejecting the organized serpent — and rejecting the unperceptive mob that is crawling with embryonic serpents.

Repeatedly, Jesus directed his strongest condemnation against those who saw him as "blaspheming" against what they viewed as "sacred" laws. His words were, "You serpents, you generation of vipers! How can you escape the

damnation of hell?"

At that time, the Jews were, and since that time have continued to be, the most conspicuous example of a serpent-group of people. The Jews were then, and are now, fanatically cohesive by reason of conformity to unifying word-dogmas. These dogmas make up their traditions, their serpent culture.

At the time the Jewish serpent was formed, dragon and serpent were very close to being interchangeable terms. Dragon was a conspicuously violent serpent. Serpent was a scheming, underhanded dragon. The same dogma-controlled group changed from serpent to dragon and back again. It took whatever form was most expedient.

Many people, such as the Iranians, East Indians, and Northern Europeans, had stories praising such dragon-slayers as Verathreghna or Indra. Their morality was built upon crushing serpents and slaying dragons. At that time the serpent culture had not enveloped the whole earth. The *possibility* of living outside serpent domination was still recognized.

Like Jesus, John the Baptist spoke against the dogma-controlled Jews and called them a generation of vipers. Centuries before, Isaiah had gone so far as to warn his own serpent-making people, "Come, my people, enter thou into thy chambers and shut thy doors about thee, until the indignation be overpast. ... the Lord with his sword shall punish leviathan the piercing serpent; even leviathan the crooked serpent; and he shall slay the dragon that is in the sea."

But on the whole the Jews were convinced that theirs was a uniquely "holy" serpent. They had a dogma that their specific serpent was created by their god, had eaten up the serpents of the Pharaoh, and in the end would eat up all other serpents. Then the Jewish serpent would rule the world.

The fact that troubled all people then, even as now, was the conspicuous ability of the serpent to destroy individual opposition. Compared to the serpent — in the areas known by those who listened to the words of Jesus — the individual appeared to have no value.

Jesus presented a concept of values solidly based upon the perceived reality of the universe. In his long range view of total reality, it was obvious that dogma-controlled groups are a perverse human practice that must pass away. He laid strong emphasis on the worth of the individual. In the long-range view he presented, the individual was greater than the dogma-controlled group. He pointed out that the creator of the universe, who he called Father, cherished the lillies of the field and the smallest sparrow. He pointed out that the creator of the universe ignored the fact that the establishment valued sparrows at two for a penny. Since the creator disregarded establishment values and was concerned with a single sparrow, how much more, Jesus said, must the Father value each human individual. He was speaking against serpent-perpetuated dogma that an individual has no value except as a functional part of a serpent.

The serpent culture is perpetuated by the conspicuous force that a serpent organization — a group obeying dogmas coming from an "authority" — can bring to bear on an individual. Those individuals, who have only a short range perspective, are convinced that the only way to destroy one serpent is by forming another to "eat it up."

Jesus taught something different. He taught that individuals should not identify with one serpent in order to fight another. Refusal to take part in the battle between serpents was not a dogma of commitment to pacifism. Jesus presented such non-participation as the strategy that individuals can use against serpents — *during the time that they are limiting their fight to exposing the stupidity of serpent-dogmas.* He made it emphatic that he was not trying to bring peace. He was offering a sword.

Perception is the major weapon for fighting dogma. While the strategy demanded it, "sword," as Jesus used the word, was a symbolic term for perception. But there came a time when his use of the word "sword" was not a symbol for something else. When he had decided that he — as a lone individual — was going to make an all-out physical confrontation of the serpents in the area, he knew his disciples might face *physical* danger. He told them, "Sell your coat and buy a sword.'' Clearly, he was talking about a real sharp-edged physical weapon for individual self-defense.

The teachings in the recorded words of Jesus are entirely clear. To make sure he would be understood he sharpened his message by *physical* confrontation of the serpent world. This confrontation resulted in his crucifixion. All his words and actions say this one thing: The way of the serpent is the way that will lead the human species to certain doom. Using one dogma-controlled group to destroy another cannot solve the problem. There is only one solution. There can be no dogma-controlled group when people know their worth as individuals. There can be no serpent if individuals — acting as individuals — refuse to let dogmatic words, coming from the law and the prophets, overrule the holy spirit within themselves.

The basic problem is still with us. The solution is still obvious. If the human species as we know it is not to perish, the dogma-controlled people, who allow themselves to be made into serpents, must be replaced by individuals who are conscious enough of the holy spirit within themselves to view the creator of the universe as their aboriginal Father.

The recorded words of Jesus are these: ''As Moses lifted up the serpent in the wilderness, even so must the son of man be lifted up, that whosoever believeth on him shall not perish, but have eternal life.''

Who first misinterpreted those words to mean that Jesus was praising the serpent?

When the torture racks of the ''Christian'' inquisition are no longer forcing everyone to accept that misinterpretation, why do so many still accept it?

Why — when the United States was founded on a proclamation declaring American Independence from all who followed the way of the serpent — do so many American ''Christians'' claim that the words of Jesus, and his submission to crucifixion, are assurance that the serpent is ''holy''?

Clearing up *this strange condition* has now become the *first* step in solving the human problem.

Chapter 2

Whether for good or ill, whether fact or fiction, the story of Jesus has had an effect — perhaps an enormous effect — in determining human destiny. In the United States there are two conspicuous views of the story. One is held by those who believe that Jesus was a "supernatural" being, that all people in the world have "sinned," and that Jesus was crucified as a sacrifice for their "sins." The other is held by those who look upon the first group as a bunch of "born-again" boobs, and wish the whole story had never got started.

From time to time, obscure writers, and some not so obscure, have presented a third viewpoint. They have said that the story of Jesus is most significant when told straight. They take the position that the "supernatural" coloring was imposed *by the enemies of Jesus*. The purpose of the enemies was to destroy the significance of the actual story. That is the viewpoint which I will examine here.

As a prelude to that examination, I present three significant facts taken from the Bible:

1. Jesus walked into his death deliberately and talked about it beforehand — but he never said he was going to die to save "sinners" from punishment.

2. Jesus used the terms god and Father interchangeably — but he never said that the god he referred to as Father was Jehovah, or Yahweh, the god of the Jews.

3. Jesus never said that he was a unique "supernatural" being, or that he had any non-natural powers. Quite the contrary. He said to his disciples: All that I do, you can do — and even greater things.

I want to amplify the last of these points. Jesus never said that his relation to the creator of the universe, which he called "the Father," was different from what others might know. Most often he referred to himself as the "son of man," while at the same time saying that all are born "children of god." I view his words as saying that a "child of man" and a "child of god" have one and the same heritage.

Now, suppose we look at the story of Jesus without assuming that Jesus was a "supernatural" being. If, as I believe, the injection of the "supernatural" was an effort of his enemies to cover up something, then his life, teachings, and crucifixion could very well mean even more if we look at the stark reality. Some questions need to be asked: Why such an effort to cover up the real story? What was unique about the crucifixion of Jesus?

At the time of Jesus, crucifixion was a very common occurrence. The cross of Jesus did not even stand alone against the darkening sky on the hill called Golgotha. There were two other crosses on the same hill that same day, two other blood dripping figures hanging beside him.

We are all familiar with the evidence that both "lawful" and "unlawful" groups have ability to overpower one individual after another that opposes the group. The groups that engage in "unlawful" mob lynchings are usually condemned without a second thought. The "lawful" ones get a little more examination. Amid the myriad crucifixions executed by "lawful" well-organized, dogma-controlled groups, why should the crucifixion of Jesus be singled out for special attention. Unquestionably it has been.

The crucifix, the manufactured image of Jesus hanging on the cross, and the myriad paintings of the pierced hands and dripping blood — these are everywhere. They arouse pity and human compassion. They point up the known fact that humans have been conditioned to practice a uniquely human viciousness, not exhibited by any other animals. But Jesus did not need to walk into his death just to show us these things. A hundred years before his crucifixion, there was a much more impressive scene.

When those who joined Spartacus in revolt against Roman

slavery were captured, over six thousand of them were crucified. A writhing, blood-dripping body was nailed to one cross after another. The crosses were placed every few feet along the Appian Way. For more miles along Rome's greatest highway than one could travel from the first light of dawn until dark obscured the pitious scene, crosses of crucified bodies stretched as far as the eye could see. No one dared take them down. No one dared wrap them in fine linen and bury them in a tomb. They hung there as a rotting, stinking repulsive warning to everyone. They were a warning of what happened to anyone who dared defy the dogma-controlled group — the dominant organized power.

These human bodies nailed to crosses for an unbelievable stretch of miles were those of the seventy Greek gladiators and six thousand slaves the gladiators tried to lead to freedom. These were the bodies of those who were captured after they had fought against fully organized Roman armies — and after they had fully defeated and turned back two such armies. The gladiator-led slaves resisted until captured.

One great difference between them and Jesus was that Jesus was not a slave; there was no greater restraint on him than on most other humans, who submit to dogma-control, then and now. Also he could have avoided the confrontation and crucifixion. He sought it out. That is not the common way, but it is not unusual. Many have deliberately sought martyrdom to gain attention for certain causes in our lifetime. The same had been done long before Jesus came along.

At the time of Jesus a four hundred year old story of voluntary martyrdom for a cause was fully documented and well known. Even now this story of the trial and execution of Socrates is still widely read. The calm, non-resistance with which Jesus faced his trial and execution was fully matched by Socrates. The Greeks, having finer sensibilities than the Jews and Romans, were much more humane in their executions. They allowed Socrates to bid a calm, extended goodby to his friends before drinking his cup of hemlock. The death Jesus faced required more courage than the one faced by Socrates. However that is not enough to make the crucifixion of Jesus unique. Even greater courage than that shown by Jesus has been shown by many others — and their stories have long been forgotten.

We must look to the significance of the *statement being made* by the martyrdom of Jesus in order to discover why this story might deserve exceptionally wide attention.

We find that obstacles have been placed so as to hide the significant. This leads to the question of why the cover up.

The story of Socrates is the older one by centuries, yet it is repeated today with total clarity. In the case of Socrates, there is little difference of opinion about what happened, and what the happening meant. If the meaning behind the crucifixion of Jesus was so significant that a great effort has been made to mutilate the story, then a great effort to rediscover that significance is warranted.

On the surface, there are striking parallels in the two stories. Like Socrates, Jesus calmly walked into the situation where he would be tried and executed by an uncomprehending people. Also, like Socrates, Jesus appeared to do this because, words failing, he saw that the total commitment of his physical being was the final, and most eloquent, statement he could make.

In both cases the populace cried for death because an individual had spoken against the dogmas of the state. In this area lies the biggest and most significant problem that uniquely confronts word-using humans. This same problem has been faced in more ways by more word-using humans than any other. The issue of individual versus state is of supreme importance to every human. The supreme importance of this issue cries out for utmost clarity.

The issue as pointed up by Socrates was not as sharply defined as when pointed up by Jesus. It contained two ambiguities. The first was in the concept of the state, itself. Dogma is usually the most conspicuous factor making up the fictitious entity now called "state" or "nation." The dogma on which the Greek state was built was that it was a "scientific state" and, as such, could avoid dogma. Therefore, in its basic concept, the Greek state was ambiguous. The second ambiguity in the issue was that Socrates clearly approved the state.

The story of Socrates drinking the hemlock has not been twisted. The probable reason is significant: Demagogs, who seek to mold masses of people into a "lawful" dogma-controlled group, have never found any need to twist it. The ambiguities that are part of the story are of use to demagogs.

Unlike the Greek city-states, the Jewish nation-state was not ambiguous. It was a classic serpent-nation. The Nomadic Jewish Nation was built upon life-and-death control of a cohesive people by the use of laws based exclusively on dogma. The dogma-controlled group tolerated no dissent. The first day the dogma was offered, Moses had three thousand killed because they would not accept the "authoritative" laws as coming from their god. The Jewish serpent dogma meant certain death for anyone who was "bitten" by other serpents — for anyone who failed to look with accepting belief on the serpent lifted up by Moses.

Unlike such "lawful" groups as the Greek city-states, where it was recognized that governments are instituted by men, the Jewish Nation claimed that its government came from a god, called Yahweh. This was not simply a different name given to the intelligence perceivable in nature. Many people call the aboriginal creative intelligence in nature "god." Jesus called that intelligence "Father." Yahweh was a fictitious god, fabricated to lend "god-authority" to unscrupulous human purposes. Moses originally made use of this primitive practice to give a god-facade to the sabotage action that the Jews were taking against the Egyptians. He obviously thought that the highly religious Egyptians would be impressed by the god-facade. Apparently they were not; they drove the Jews out.

Moses then took on the task of making a full-fledged serpent. He used the classic methods that primitive serpent-makers had been using since long before the dawn of history. He used unperceptive people, acting as a group, to destroy perceptive individuals.

His precise methods sharpen the sometimes vague view we have of the direction taken by this primitive routine. He declared that the laws he enforced on the people of the Nomadic Jewish Nation came from the purported god, Yahweh, in human words. His dogma declared that disobedience was not simply violation of ordinary laws. Disobedience to these laws of the Jewish Nation was given a special name: "Sin." The invention of "sin," an emotionally-charged dogma for triggering fanatical hatred, was a unique contribution of Judaism to the primitive practice of serpent-making.

Upon the word "sin" the connotation of an *incomprehensible* guilt was overlaid. Clear comprehension was deliberately clouded over; the emotional impact of the connotation was constantly increased. Various practices accomplished these ends. The killing of individual "sinners" by dogma-drugged mobs hurling stones — with fanatical hate inflaming their eyes and the vilest curses twisting their mouths in grotesque distortion — was one such practice. Another came from the dogma that "sin" required gory, blood-letting sacrifices of everyone's first born and finest to satisfy the incomprehensible needs or wishes of the wrathful god Yahweh — apparently a fictitious surrogate Pharaoh.

Like calling the violation of law "sin," treason was also given an emotional connotation and called "blasphemy." The connotations imposed on these words were designed to impress upon the unperceptive that the Jewish "Pharaoh" was not Moses but a "supernatural" lawmaker whose needs, wishes, and purposes could not be understood by ordinary people. Specially "inspired" priests and prophets were required to "explain" the ways of Yahweh.

At the time of Jesus, there had been more than twelve centuries for this man-made "supernatural" culture to overrule the natural selection that favors survival of the perceptive. The unperceptive selected to survive and bear children by this man-made culture lived in an atmosphere of "sin," "blasphemy," "sacrifice," and attempted obedience to the laws from an incomprehensible "god." The confused atmosphere clouded the vision of those who had eyes to see, and the comprehension of those who had ears to hear.

Onto this confusion of the people, circumstances had added another confusion. The Jewish serpent had come under the power of the Romans. The people, who were both culturally bred and environmentally conditioned for lack of perception, were caught between two powers both claiming absolute "authority."

Into the midst of these people, Jesus was born. Like all the others, he was caught between the overt force of the Roman serpent, and the secret, underhanded, anti-Roman plotting that constantly went on within the Jewish serpent. Like all others, he was under constant pressure to choose between them. But, unlike most others, Jesus did not want to choose between them. He saw both serpents as equally abhorrent.

Unlike most who had been bred for lack of perception, Jesus was uniquely perceptive. He saw the *very practice* of serpent-making as a totally unacceptable mutilation of the human species. He clearly perceived wherein lay the only salvation of all mankind.

The way of human salvation, the way of nature and nature's god, was clear to Jesus. The only problem was how to point it out to the people among whom he was born. There was no thought pattern in the area that oriented on nature and nature's god.

At first he tried to deal exclusively in the thought pattern of the Jews. It is this highly-accented, classically-primitive thought pattern that provided the fullest contrast to his teachings. The complex of confused dogmas faced his clear perception with a morass that closed in almost as fast as he made a path.

The "supernatural" ("above" nature) source, claimed for the dogmas of the Nomadic Jewish Nation, was obviously designed to thwart any appeal to reason. It was successful. The confused, emotionally-charged, semi-concept of "sin" could not be faced directly.

Jesus said to numerous people "your sins are forgiven." This was frequently taken as meaning that he had some special power to forgive "sins." Perceptive people would, of course, have recognized the inference that "sin" was a meaningless word.

Let us look at a specific example. Jesus was confronted by a mob that had found a woman committing adultery and was preparing to stone her to death in accordance with the laws of Moses. He wrote on the ground, while he pondered how to save her. Finally he said, "He who is without sin among you, let him first cast a stone at her." It might be interpreted that he dispersed the mob with these words because he knew all had "sinned." The perceptive would realize that he acted on the knowledge that all who believed the woman had "sinned" were deluded by a mob-controlling dogma — and control of the mob required that he use the handle that dogma-makers had fashioned for mob control. The total evidence of his teachings clearly indicates that he merely used the dogma-controlled-mob's own madness to protect the woman.

After it could be seen that Jesus was trying to find a way to break through the people's conditioned thought pattern, the dogma-indoctrinated people began to recognize that he was not one of them. Some, who thought themselves very clever in tangling others in arguments where they thought they had more knowledge, repeatedly confronted Jesus. They tried to trap him into making statements that were clearly treasonous (or "blasphemous"). They wanted *evidence* that he was opposing the "sin"-designating laws, which Moses claimed had actually been written on stone by god. Jesus parried their efforts to accuse him of treason without expressing agreement with the dogmatic semi-concept of "sin."

One of the many confusing points which came from the purportedly god-given laws was the one regarding adultery. This highly important subject will need some extensive examination when we talk of biological regression. It is, therefore, appropriate to look further at what Jesus said about it.

If Jesus could have spoken freely, that is, if he could have spoken without triggering the accusation of "blasphemy" before he thought the time was ripe for it, he might have put a significant question to his interrogators. He might have questioned whether it was lack of intelligence or under-handed scheming that prompted a commandment saying "Thou shalt not commit adultery" — when "adultery" could have no meaning unless a commandment defining "marriage" was first set forth.

The dogmas of a group which arrogates to itself the "authority" to sanction marriage, or decide what constitutes "adultery," always mutilate perception of nature and nature's god in some way. The dogma of the Jewish Nation, "Thou shalt not commit adultery" — which veiled the underlying dogmas regarding marriage — was among the trickiest Jesus had to face. He met it head-on by saying that "one who looks on a woman to lust after her has committed adultery with her in his heart already."

Jesus had to pick his words very carefully in order to talk to those who had eyes to see but saw not. In this case, he could perceive that, in their dogma-drugged minds, "lust," as distinguished from love, was a perverted emotion resulting from the "adultery" dogma. "Lust" had the same emotional connotation as "adultery." An aversion to "lust," as distinguished from love, might have been a point of understanding between Jesus and those who had an emotional acceptance of a dogma regarding "adultery"; however, the emotional cloud surrounding the dogma, itself, made any appeal to reason impossible.

Although dogma was so strong that he could make no direct appeal to reason, Jesus never confirmed the prevalent idea that *failure to conform to group-enforced dogma* regarding marriage, adultery, or anything else was "sin."

Repeatedly Jesus said, "Your sins are forgiven." But only those who have eyes to see and see not, ears to hear and hear not, could take those words as intended to perpetuate the confused, psychotic complex-of-ideas-and-emotions brought forward by the word "sin."

One who assures children that no ghosts or goblins will get them does not thereby confirm the existence of ghosts and goblins. To further comfort children one might add, "There are no such things as ghosts and goblins." But Jesus knew that his ability to teach the people would come to an abrupt end if he said plainly, "There is no such thing as sin." In Jewish practice, "sin" was the most distinguishing tradition.

Jesus never confirmed the dogma-implanted conviction of the people that they were guilty of the "sins" of Adam. He never confirmed their belief that failure to obey the laws that Moses said came from their god was "sin." Nothing he ever said would confirm the present day belief of "Christians" that he was sent into the world to die for their "sins."

If we look only at the teachings of Jesus — and not at the teachings of Paul — there is no evidence that the god whom Jesus called "Father" ever required, or wanted, any human, or any god, or any beast to be sacrificed to save anyone from "sin."

For those who have eyes to read for themselves, and ears to hear what is actually being read, the gospel according to Jesus is this: "The law and the prophets were until John. You can transgress against what men call law and be forgiven, you can transgress against what men call god and be forgiven, but if you transgress against the holy spirit within you, you will not be forgiven in the dogma-dominated world that exists now, nor in the world that is to come."

Jesus recognized that if the human species is to survive, it will survive in a new world, where groups can no longer enforce dogma on individuals.

First he offered salvation to the Jews. When it was rejected — when he recognized that "the new wine would break the old bottles" — he made his final and most eloquent statement. The crystal clarity of that statement is greater than any ever made before or since.

Before the Romans, Jews, and all the peoples of the world, Jesus confronted the most clearly defined serpent known to history. The serpent could not avoid the open confrontation. Jesus initiated it.

He had not triggered the hostility of any of the serpent's fanatical mobs that killed by stoning against some back alley wall. He had not "sinned" against any specific one of the serpent's dogmas. Instead, he brought the "holiness" of all those dogmas into question. In public view and under Roman power those who acted on instructions purportedly coming from a god using human words could not eliminate Jesus in the way Moses had eliminated the first three thousand who denied the "holiness" of the serpent's laws.

Roman rule over the Jews included a court that gave some semblance of a public hearing. There, Jesus, as one individual, could stand in contrast to the Jewish serpent, and the whole world could "read" the statement made by that physical confrontation.

He was guilty of nothing that any group called "crime."

He could be accused of nothing but faithfulness to the god within himself. Because he had so lived that no other accusation could be made, there was no cloud on his clear statement.

One physical individual — a sovereign descendant of the universal creative intelligence, unconditioned by dogma — stood alone against the most clearly defined serpent known to history. Before all mankind, the crucifixion of Jesus proclaimed the mortal opposition that eternally exists in that relationship.

He chose his time carefully. He went into Jerusalem when all were celebrating the feast of the passover. The passover feast was the "holiest" Jewish tradition, supposedly commanded by Yahweh whom Moses claimed spoke to him in human words. It was the birthday of the Nomadic Jewish Nation as an embryonic serpent. It was the time when Jews proclaimed to each other that their god, who purportedly loved one serpent and no other, had promised them that the Jewish serpent would eventually dominate the world.

Jesus begain his final statement when, *at the time for the passover feast,* he ate his last supper with his disciples. Moses had said that his god commanded that the ritual passover meal be eaten "standing — with your shoes on your feet." Jesus had his disciples sit. He made his non-conformity to the "holy law," supposedly issued by the god of Moses, doubly conspicuous by washing his disciples' feet.

Then he went forth into the garden to await those he knew would come to crucify him.

The actual facts regarding the crucifixion of Jesus are the most familiar story in the world.

It would be impossible to make a statement more clear than that made by Jesus. The creative intelligence of the universe uses no human words. The real god speaks in a language where the "words" are realities. The supreme statement made by Jesus, with his very being, set up one reality in contrast to another. Jesus, as one sovereign individual, stood up in opposition to all the dogma-drugged people who are committed to the way of the serpent. All who had eyes to see could see — and choose.

The human species is not born blind. The clear statement Jesus made has been covered with a cloud. As a result, those who call themselves ''Christians'' do not hold up Jesus on the cross to show his mortal opposition to the serpent Moses lifted up in the wilderness. They hold up the crucified Jesus in an effort to confirm that the serpent which Jesus condemned is ''holy.''

What happened?

An anti-Christ, called Paul, used human words to recrucify Jesus.

CHAPTER 3

The very word 'Christianity' is a misunderstanding — at bottom there was only one Christian, and he died on the cross. What, from that moment onward, was called the 'Gospels' was the very reverse of what *he* had lived. In Paul is incarnated the very opposite of the 'bearer of glad tidings'; he represents the genius for hatred. *What*, indeed, has not this dysangelist sacrificed to hatred! Above all, the Savior; he nailed him to *his own* cross. . . .Once more the priestly instinct of the Jew perpetuated the same old master crime against history — he simply struck out the yesterday and the day before yesterday of Christianity, and *invented his own history of Christian beginnings.* — What *he* wanted was power; in Paul the priest once more reached out for power — he had use only for such concepts, teachings and symbols as served the purpose of tyrannizing over the masses and organizing mobs.

The Antichrist — **Friedrich Nietzsche**

Long before the time of Jesus, the word "serpent" meant: The controlled people who act as a unit. The people, themselves, who made up a "serpent" were, of course, realities. The concept carried by the word was abstract and complex. However, in general use, there was nothing "supernatural" about a "serpent."

While the Jews were making themselves into a serpent, they began — and still continue — trying to confuse language and rewrite world history. They imposed the "supernatural" connotation on the word "serpent" in an attempt to confuse its meaning. They obviously did this because they did not want the word to have the usual unfavorable connotation when used to designate the Nomadic Jewish Nation. The use of the word, itself could not be avoided; the word and its meaning were too well known.

Long before the Jews became a serpent, an old Babylonian story told about two lovers in a paradise-like garden, whose idealistic happiness was destroyed by a serpent. The serpent lured them away from their private paradise by the promise of a better life. The story was a simplified telling of a commonplace experience when "civilizations" were embryos. Most "civilizations" were becoming serpents. A great *conscious* effort was needed to overcome the primitive practice. Everyone recognized that the story was setting forth the foremost human problem. Everyone knew the story and repeated it.

Long before Jesus was born, the Jews — or those among them who survived the slaughter Moses said had been ordered by god — chose to make themselves into a serpent. In an effort to avoid the unfavorable connotation attached to "serpent," they modified the widespread Babylonian story. They presented the two lovers as being the first man and woman on earth. Of course, with such a twist, the accepted meaning of serpent could not apply. To adapt the long cherished story to their own use, they presented the serpent as a magic sort of biological reptile that talked in human words. They presented it as something "supernatural" — as a devil. Then, to make their own serpent-nation look favorable, they fictionalized an opposing "supernatural" power — a "good guy," a god, Yahweh — who they claimed had created the Jewish serpent to eat up other serpents.

With these twists, they adopted the old, long repeated story. The Jewish Bible described the "sin" of listening to the serpent, of accepting the serpent doctrine that there could be a good and evil different from that manifest in nature. However, the "sin" that lost those who listened to the serpent their position in paradise was blamed on past generations. It was presented as beyond the power of present generations to rectify. Unquestioned acceptance of serpent ways was presented as "acceptance of the way things are." It was so presented because the Jews, after being driven out of Egypt and finding themselves free to choose their own way of life, did not want to abandon the perverted serpent culture and return to nature.

At the time of Jesus, the Romans controlled the Jews. Around the area occupied by the Jews, the Romans also controlled thirteen cities that Alexander the Great had set up to teach Greek thought and the Greek way of life to others. The maelstrom of incompatible ideas under Roman control made for confusion. Efforts to interpret the teachings of Jesus contributed to the existing confusion. Confusion prepares the ground for dogma.

In the area were many who had long been dogma-controlled and who had learned how to use dogma for control of others. It was a generation of vipers — of little, highly poisonous word-twisters, aspiring to become serpent-makers. They had a fertile field in which to test their ambitions.

After the crucifixion of Jesus, various groups drew together for mutual support. They needed it. Their efforts to adapt their way of life to the ideas of *individual* human worth, that Jesus had proclaimed, required a lot of new thinking. Some groups were infiltrated by serpent and dragon makers. Often, the infiltrated groups opposed each other. All faced opposition from the fully established serpents.

Within the first century after the crucifixion of Jesus, there were at least a hundred separate groups who were called "Christians." In 303 A.D. a Christian soldier called George, who had gained a wide reputation as a dragon slayer, was captured, tortured and killed by the Roman Emperor Diocletian. Seeing that Christians were becoming dragon-slayers, as the unconquerable German warriors to the north had always been, the Romans began to take official notice. In 314 A.D. the Roman Emperor Constantine, impressed by the growing power of some groups calling themselves Christians, convened a council to study their teachings. At a subsequent council in 325 A.D. he selected the followers of certain doctrines for official approval —

with the understanding that they would either absorb or destroy the others. Those selected were the ones whose dogma came from the group that, over two hundred years before, had been taken over by Paul (Saul of Tarsus).

In direct opposition to the teachings of Jesus, Paul had laid a solid foundation for making this specific group into a serpent. The serpent foundation was laid by twisting everything known about Jesus backwards, so as to make it support Jewish dogma. Paul — not Jesus, and not Peter — was the founder of the church that brought about all the horror of the inquisitions and all the witch burnings that took place in the name of "Christianity."

Paul (Saul of Tarsus) was a double agent. He posed as both Paul, a Roman citizen, and Saul, a fully committed citizen of the Nomadic Jewish Nation. Opposition to those who had accepted the teachings of Jesus provided a unique opportunity for a double agent, normally working in secret, to gain *public* acclaim. The new Christians claimed individual sovereignty and rejected all serpent dogma. Both Romans and Jews wanted to exterminate them. Paul was given license from the Romans, and encouragement from the Jews, to kill off any Christians wherever he found them. He led a bloody band that killed with Jewish hatred and Roman efficiency; as a Jew or as a Roman, killing Christians seemed the only way to deal with them.

The final statement of Jesus had been a reality. Those who accepted and followed the teachings of Jesus were realities. At first, Paul, as an instrument of the serpents, used a sword as the only possible argument against those who had learned the language of reality and no longer accepted dogmas.

However, as Paul went about his bloody job, the accumulated education of a people who prided themselves on their use of words to distort reality churned in his mind. He searched for some clever idea. At last, he was virtually struck dumb and blind by his own brilliance. He had thought of a way to twist the remembered reality of the crucifixion so as to give it an exactly opposite meaning. He would make the very crucifixion of Jesus proclaim that the god invented by Moses was a reality. He would call the crucifixion of Jesus a god-intended substitute-punishment for the "sins" of others. There were numerous precedents in the Jewish tradition. It could work! *And he had the force already in his hands to get it started.*

Paul was on his way to kill a group of Christians when — according to the story he told — he had a vision of Jesus that persuaded him to quit persecuting Christians. Regardless of any vision seen by Paul, the known facts are unmistakable: Paul did not accept the teachings of Jesus; he manipulated those who had accepted those teachings so as to destroy all Christians more effectively than he could have done with a sword. He nailed Jesus on the cross a second time. He called the crucified Jesus a new edition of the prototype Moses had lifted up in the wilderness. In lieu of killing the followers of Jesus, he made them into a new embryonic serpent after the Jewish pattern. Then he spent the rest of his life diametrically reversing the teachings of Jesus.

The core of Paul's new anti-Christ "Christianity" was identifying the figure of Jesus on the cross with the bloody sacrifices prescribed by the monstrous god invented by Moses. This was designed to perpetuate the dogma that the Jewish serpent was "holy," that the Nomadic Jewish Nation was created by god, that the Jewish laws were delivered to the Jews by god, and that those laws were intended for the rule of the whole world.

This was a lot to swallow for those who had, themselves, known, or had known someone who had known, Jesus. But according to Paul, acceptance of Jesus as a sacrificial substitute for one's own "sins" would be the only way to join Jesus in the "kingdom of heaven" he had talked about. Paul now said that this kingdom of heaven existed *after* death. The idea — after death — might have come to Paul from some vicious remark made in his bloody band about sending the followers of Jesus to join their king in his kingdom of heaven. However, there were enough confused stories about Jesus to make it possible to twist the "kingdom of heaven" words of Jesus so as to interpret them as referring to an after-death kingdom "for all holy spirits." Paul's basic task was to make Christian groups accept the dogma that — on earth — they way of the serpent *must be accepted* as "the way things are."

As it had done for fifteen hundred years, once more the culture of the Jews produced a serpent-maker. As Jewish priests had always done, so Paul did now. He used words to strike out the history of what is reality — and invent a new history that served his own purpose. He was a serpent-maker; he wanted only the concepts, teachings and symbols that could be used to organize and manipulate mobs.

Serpent-makers cherish and perpetuate the word-distortions-of-reality that are the tools of their trade. The 325 A.D. council of those seeking approval of the Emperor Constantine updated Paul's plan for destroying Christianity in a way that was more effective than simply killing Christians. The new generation of anti-Christ planners placed strong emphasis on miracles that had been ascribed Jesus. As a "supernatural" clincher, they injected a new story that Jesus was born of a virgin. They changed the birth date to coincide with the existing winter solstice festival. Planning to use the Christian movement, itself, to destroy the teachings of Jesus, they left much of the actual stories and recorded words of Jesus unchanged. Because they built upon the foundation that Paul had laid, there was no need to change them. The contrary was true. As Paul had twisted some of the meanings, the actual words of Jesus became useful to serpent makers. Paul had twisted the meaning so as to make non-participation in the fight between serpents, which had been presented as a strategy by Jesus, into a dogma of total non-violence. Such a dogma could be very useful to an emperor who wanted docile subjects. Also, by the diabolically clever twist of meaning Paul had given to the crucifixion, Paul's "Christianity" carried forward the full "supernatural" fanaticism of Judaism. He presented the amalgam as saying that the Jewish serpent was a "holy" prototype of that crucifixion. Thus Jesus-on-the-cross was to be made into a "holy" *serpent-symbol.*

The ambiguous "supernatural" meaning that the Jews had imposed on the word "serpent" would be made more ambiguous. The Nomadic Jewish Nation would, of course, no longer be called a serpent. And the "Christian" serpent would, of course, be given a name other than serpent. It would be called the Holy Roman Church.

The "Christianity" teachings that became the dogmas of the Roman-church-serpent were the teachings of Paul, the anti-Christ. The church canonized Paul, gave him the designation of Saint Paul, and made the letters he had written to his chain of churches part of what came to be called the "Holy" Bible.

Even after the 325 A.D. Council at Nice had worked over the gospels as written by Matthew, Mark, Luke, and John, the difference between the teachings of Jesus and the teachings of Paul, as both appear in the Bible, are still conspicuous to anyone who looks for them.

The joyous tidings Jesus brought to all Jews, who had ears to hear, was that Jewish law was a contemptible concoction promoted by hypocritical scribes and Pharisees — and that disobedience to that law was nothing but disobedience to serpent dogma — not "sin."

Paul reiterated the Jewish dogma that all are born "sinners," guilty of the "sins" of their fathers, guilty of the "sins" of Adam.

The god that Jesus called "Father" was the actual creative intelligence of the universe, the god of nature, the god who clothed the lillies of the field and cherished the smallest sparrow, the god who loves even the word-using humans and "listens" to prayers — if the words come from the depths of one's being. The idea which Jesus presented was that of a father who listens to his confused children when the come to him in private with a sincere desire to get understanding.

The god of Paul was the false god invented by Moses, a non-natural god, a dogma-giving god, a god purportedly commanding men to commit atrocities that no non-word-controlled animal would commit, a god who purportedly dealt with people as groups — groups that dominated the individuals who composed them, that waged war on other groups, or infiltrated and destroyed other groups by underhanded methods.

Jesus taught that the law and the prophets were until John, that transgression against dogmas coming from what people thought of as a word-using god was not a serious

thing, that nothing was important except the failure of each individual to faithfully identify with the holy spirit within. He taught that the kingdom of god and the kingdom of heaven are the kingdoms known to be possible because they exist as something within, something different from "the way things are" — and, therefore, everyone's prayer should be, "Thy kingdom come, thy will be done, on earth as it is in heaven."

Jesus said the "kingdom of heaven is not here and not there. Lo! The kingdom of heaven is within you."

Paul taught that the kingdom of god and the kingdom of heaven are something that can only be known after death by those who conform to the dogmas he presented. He re-emphasized the Jewish dogma that the way things now exist on earth — the way of the serpent — must be accepted as "the way things are." He taught the Jewish dogma that all serpents other than the Jewish serpent were *evil* — because they are created by men. He taught that god, himself, had created the Jewish serpent to eat up the others. Therefore the Jewish serpent, unlike all the others, was "holy."

Jesus knew that "holy" serpent and "unholy" serpent were meaningless words. Looking at life's realities, he perceived that there was one way of life for a sovereign individual of the human species — a "son of man" in his language — and another way of life as a functional part of a serpent. The two ways went in opposite directions. He perceived that salvation of the human species requires *full* condemnation of serpents — the "holy" along with the "unholy."

Jesus perceived that those who used dogma-controlled mobs as weapons could drown out the mere words of any individual who made a positive statement that the Jewish serpent was not "holy." He knew that mere words from an individual would be shouted down by the conditioned hatred exploding from a multi-throated mob. He perceived that a clear, lasting statement would require more than human words.

Jesus made his very being into the language of his Father, nature's god, whose words are realities. He walked into the situation where the serpent-people would crucify him for no

reason except that he had proclaimed his individual sovereignty. He knew that he had so lived that the serpent people could accuse him of nothing except that he had been true to himself. By confronting them, and forcing them to speak the language of reality, he brought into sharp focus the reality of those that follow serpent ways: They demand more than abstinence from "criminal" behavior; they demand absolute control of everyone's words and thoughts; they demand control of the holy spirit within; they demand that no son of man be allowed to live who does not identify with a serpent. Forcing them to make that statement by raising upon a cross the blood-dripping, spit-upon figure of one, who had done nothing but be true to himself, was the supremely eloquent condemnation Jesus made of serpent ways.

Jesus said of the Roman soldiers who nailed him to the cross, "Father, forgive them, they know not what they do."

But, from the words of Jesus, there is another quote for the many calling themselves "Christians" who continue nailing him to that cross: "Depart from me, you workers of iniquity; I never knew you."

CHAPTER 4

If Christianity — instead of the teachings of Jesus twisted backwards — had been introduced into Northern Europe, the contrast to what did happen could have been staggering. The heaven on earth that could have developed by now would fulfill the finest dream. It was the dream that had taken hold of Jesus.

The predictions of Jesus were entirely realistic. We look back and discover that the closeness the human species came to achieving *that utterly different world he visualized* is amazing. Suppose we look at what might have been. Suppose we place the significant teachings of Jesus — instead of the teachings of Paul — in the same historical perspective.

Somewhere back before recorded history — maybe even a hundred thousand years ago, the unscrupulous use of dogma-controlled groups to destroy strong, perceptive individuals began to supplant natural selection. This human-culture-of-humans began determining the direction of the human species.

Among primitive peoples, the "authority" of the serpent-maker is often based on group acceptance that there is something outside of nature that the witch doctors know. The credulous, awed by the witch doctor's claim to "super" natural power, accept his instructions to kill perceptive dissenters who point out what the unscrupulous witch doctors are doing.

Because there is no criterion of reality by which to measure a purported "supernatural" instruction-giver, primitive people fight endlessly over which of their inventions, their non-natural gods, is the "one true god." Since no basis for agreement can ever exist, eternal mass warfare is an inevitable consequence of serpents based on "supernatural" dogma. The Nomadic Jewish Nation is the best known example of a nation founded on this perverted culture that breeds out the perceptive and propagates the unscrupulous.

Beginning with the Jews' clandestine poisoning of the Egyptian cattle and first born children, and their subsequent agreement of how they would tell the story, the Old Testament is a gory record of typical primitive war and underhanded sabotage — purportedly directed by a "supernatural" god.

Condemnation of Judaism — formalized primitivism — was what made the crucifixion of Jesus into a significant statement.

A "supernatural" god is not an essential factor in developing a group culture that destroys dissenting individuals. However a culture based on a "supernatural" god points up most sharply the peculiarly human factor of group control by the use of words. And it is the one that played havoc in the Western world.

In the Orient, expanding families evolved into great numbers, organized themselves into group powers based on parental "authority" and became dragons. Without "supernatural" dogma, the Chinese and Japanese have always accepted the dragon as an inevitable human development — as "the way things are." They have always taken it in their stride. The paper dragon, moved by many individuals underneath it, is a standard part of their festivals. In their parades, the paper image feigns vicious attacks on individuals, and individuals feign both terror and taunting of the dragon. At festival season, it is good fun. In everyday life, the fear is often very real, and blood sometimes flows like rivers.

The fragments indicating the main stream of Western history about four or five thousand years before Jesus show that many Western people had evolved beyond the "supernatural" that characterizes the most primitive peoples. The pre-Jewish Babylonian story of two lovers tempted by a serpent was a clear and simple statement that groupism is the major threat to individual sovereignty. The story showed that the serpent was especially threatening to the sovereignty of a male and female in expressing their maleness and femaleness, in choosing their own mates, and in creating their own paradise.

The Aryans, or Iranians as the word is now spelled, the people on the Iranian plateau north of Babylon, made a positive commitment to individual sovereignty. They went further than merely pointing out the major threat named in the Babylonian story. They pointed out the solution. They told stories about individuals who became dragon slayers. The stories praised the dragon slayers as examples of the highest morality.

We have no exact history telling how numerous were these early Aryan people who rejected the serpent-dragon primitivism and made a full commitment to the slaying of dragons. At the time of our first historical fragments they had given their name, the name that now merely designates their language, to the Iranian plateau. We do not know precisely what areas other than Europe and the Iranian plateau they dominated four or five thousand years before Jesus. We do know that, at the time of Jesus, they had already taken two different social paths in two different areas.

Those in India had gone the way of trying to co-exist with the natives. They tried to educate the natives to their way of life, based on individual sovereignty.

Those in Northern Europe insisted on complete segregation. They took pride in keeping a no-man's land between themselves and the people of the Mediterranean who continued the serpent-dragon culture. Northern Europe was a formidable fortress for individual sovereignty and dragon slayers.

The oldest known artifacts of metal working have been found in Europe. Apparently, by the time of Jesus, the Northern Europeans had already passed through, and left behind, the passion for accumulating possessions. Apparently their culture had progressed beyond the dependence on the artifacts by which serpent-trained historians rate "civilizations." Clearly they had rejected the mass-breeding of dogma-controlled workers, which characterize "civilizations" that measure status by accumulated possessions.

The Romans had thrust a passage all the way to the British Isles, across the area called Gaul. However, Rome's finest armies were never able to make any substantial penetration into the heartland of Northern Europe.

In Gaul, they had made a beginning toward imposing serpent ways on the people. The Romans were turning Greek art into "supernatural" dogma and using it as a serpent-making tool.

Before they were conquered by the Romans, the Aryan Greeks, who kept primitive peoples as slaves, had created a pantheon of "gods." The Greeks fully understood that their "gods" were fictional, *artistic* creations. As mentioned before, the Greek state was an ambiguous concept. It tried to go half-way toward co-existence with the primitives. It accepted and made use of slaves and, at the same time, intellectually rejected the serpent way of life. The distinction between "art" and "supernatural" got confused.

Among themselves, the Romans took over the "gods" of the Greek pantheon as little more than a new social fad. They imposed them upon the conquered Gauls as the "religion" of the conquering dragon. They demanded that this "religion" be accepted as the "supernatural" source of Roman dogma.

The Saxons and other unconquered Germanic tribes at the heart of Northern Europe clearly had no non-natural gods. They had been totally non-primitive, and uncontrolled by dogma, for thousands of years. They looked upon natural realities as being the language of the universal creative intelligence. They "read" the language of the universal creative intelligence as it is written in nature. Their morality accepted the direction pointed by nature. They based all inter-personal and social relationships on a conscious commitment to the sovereignty of the individual.

All individuals were free to express the creative spirit born within them by word — and by action — as individuals. Social approval of *individual action* was made into a conscious discipline that bred out demagogs. It bred out those who sought to distort individual perception of the spirit within and create a dogma-controlled group-dragon. Confronting and killing dragon-makers was recognized as a moral act and a public benefit — not a "sin" or "crime."

The Northern Europeans accepted at face value the abundant evidence that the aboriginal creative intelligence had not *created* organic life as an amusing plaything external to the aboriginal creative being. They viewed everything in nature as evidence that the aboriginal creative intelligence had *become* organic life. They concluded that all individuals — human and non-human — were therefore born sovereign individuals and, *as individuals,* had the capacity and need to express the creative intelligence within themselves in action. Their social structure based all non-combative relationships on agreements between individuals, who recognized that *all were equally sovereign.*

Such a social structure is incomprehensible to primitive serpent peoples. Serpent people know only two kinds of "individualism" — (1) Animal instinct, and (2) the condition called "anarchy," which is the psychotic *reaction* to organized human serpent-madness. They have no concept of a truly civilized way of life based on individual sovereignty. They have no concept of what it means to discard the primitive social structure built upon "possessions" and upon "positions of authority." They have no concept of what is involved in becoming civilized enough to respect nature as the vital continuity of the aboriginal creative intelligence. They have no concept of the human potential as a conscious expression of that vital continuity. They have not perceived the "kingdom of heaven" that is within them.

In the view of the early Northern Europeans a socio-religious-political group of people that presently is called a nation-state was either (1) based upon agreements between sovereign individuals, or (2) based upon dogma-control of individuals by manipulators, who fight — in a dishonorable, underhanded way — among themselves for control of groups. The Northern Europeans recognized that the practice destroys perceptive individuals. They recognized the whole system as being the greatest possible crime against the human species.

The Northern Europeans wanted no relations with serpent people. Except for those who used the story of Jesus as a false passport, they allowed no intruders across their no-man's land.

At first they viewed the priests, telling the story of Jesus, as similar to their own wandering troubadours. They did not recognize the kindly appearing priests as invaders. Always before, serpent-people had invaded as dragons. As dragons, they were met and destroyed.

The Northern European way of life was, of course, not remotely understood by serpent people. It was very little known until known by those fully pre-committed to its destruction. The few stories that have been preserved — such as Beowulf, the Islandic Eddas, and the Nibelungenlied — all passed through the hands of the Judaeo-"Christians" who were as intent on reversing their meaning as Paul was in reversing the teachings of Jesus.

Against intense opposition from the present day serpent-controlled media, the way of life *that consciously rejected all serpents and dragons* is now being slowly restated. Richard Wagner examined all the mutilated fragments with the perception of a creative artist. Like putting together enough shards of broken pottery to indicate the shape of an original vase, he rearranged, in their meaningful patterns, the subconscious symbols that expressed the early Northern European way of life. Melvin Gorham brought Wagner's works into full, present day, waking consciousness in his *Curse of the Ring* and *The Ring Cycle.* John Masefield embodied some of the Northern European though patterns bred into him in his *Sonnets.* Robinson Jeffers, in many of his works, such as *Tower Beyond Tragedy, Birth of a New Age,* and *The Double Axe,* both consciously and intuitively recreated in words the early Northern European viewpoints. John Harland, in his *Word Controlled Humans*, had shown the identity that basically existed between the teachings of Jesus and the early Northern European way of life. But on the whole, all the people of Northern European heritage have been deprived, not only of their *way of life*, but of all knowledge of it. All that is widely known is the heroism of the Vikings when they made their last stand fights. The culture that produced these heroes, and all the Northern Europeans — the people of love and honor, instead of lust and treachery — has been derogated as "savagery" by the controlled media. In the media, animal instinct and psychotic anarchy are called "individualism" — and "individualism" is dismissed as an impractical social concept. The result is a moral vacuum.

The words and actions of Jesus cannot provide a guide to a way of life different from that developed by serpent people. Because Jesus was living among people who had no concept of a way of life built upon individual sovereignty, he could not *demonstrate* interpersonal and social relations based upon individual sovereignty. Also his teachings in words — if he had tried to draw a word picture of such a social organization — would have been so utterly foreign to serpent trained people that they would have ridiculed him as a fool. All he could say was, "The kingdom of heaven is within you." As an example of his difficulty, note how people — even today — are puzzled by the fact that Jesus praised John the Baptist (who also condemned the "generation of vipers") and then said that the least in the kingdom of heaven would be greater than John.

The Northern European way of life prior to the anti-Christ Judaeo-"Christianity" of Paul would be the kingdom of heaven as extrapolated from the teachings of Jesus. If the Northern Europeans had been limited to prayers as the only possible substitute for action, they would have needed no instructions to pray to *nature's* god, "Thy will be done on earth as it is in heaven." That was the impulse behind their *actions* as individual sovereigns.

The story of Jesus became a passport across the no-man's land. It was a passport falsely used by serpent makers. The story served as a passport because the Northern Europeans already had total understanding of the teachings of Jesus.

The Northern Europeans had come to the same conclusions as Jesus thousands of years before. They recognized the same god of nature that Jesus called "Father" as the creator of the universe. They thought of themselves as direct descendants of the aboriginal creative intelligence. They cherished the vital continuity within themselves, and respected this same vital continuity (called "holy spirit" by Jesus) in others. "Government" among them consisted of personal agreements between themselves. They accepted no authority over themselves to which they had not — each individually — agreed. They recognized no "supernatural" or non-natural god. They had eyes to see and could see that the language of nature's god was not human words; it was tangible realities. No word dogmas came from, or could come from, their god. Also they postulated no "scientific" reason for "group authority" over individuals within the group, as the Greeks had done. In his commentaries, Julius Caesar recites their practice of individual sovereignty as something almost unbelievable in view of their formidable, well coordinated opposition to Roman armies. Caesar could never quite understand it, but he respected it.

Individually they were all dragon slayers. The Roman armies could not enter their area. It was only the kindly appearing priests, bearing the story of Jesus, who managed to penetrate their Northern European defenses. The story of Jesus appealed to them because they admired courage and individual integrity. As they saw the story, Jesus had accepted crucifixion in order to graphically portray to the serpent-people, among whom he was born, the simple fact to which all Northern Europeans had been fully committed for centuries. They saw Jesus as one intelligent individual born among a group of unscrupulous primitives.

As things actually happened, the only people which history records as having been selectively bred by the culture of individual sovereignty were tricked into spreading the primitive serpent way of life — the dogma of the Jews which Paul brought forward into "Christianity" — over the entire earth.

The salvation of the human species would have needed only a small change in what happened.

Suppose the Northern Europeans, who readily recognized dragons, had been wise to surreptitious serpent ways. The priests, with their false passports, would have gotten nowhere.

Or — better — suppose the true followers of Jesus had

been the ones who crossed the no-man's land. They could have taught the Northern Europeans how to handle serpents. Then suppose the Northern Europeans — who already knew full well how to handle dragons — had gone through the breached no-man's land to support the real Christians in the Mediterranean. The earth would now have become the kingdom of heaven that Jesus visualized. The difference between "things as they are" and "things as they might very easily have been" seems to have been made up of very little.

The kingdom of heaven is not an unrealistic dream.

CHAPTER 5

Serpent cultures have thousands of faces; the objective never varies. All aim at using a group to dominate dissenting individuals. Judaism is the most conspicuous serpent culture.

Scholars who have studied Jewish culture and want to be kind summarize its objective as "victory over nature." That is a distortion of the reality. Group "victory" over dissenting individuals is not "victory over nature." Viewed from the long perspective of nature, serpent culture is an attempt to create a new organic entity — a group entity. That is not victory over nature. Nature has abundant precedents for the place humans will occupy if the human species continues the direction it is now going. If the serpent culture is "victorious" humans will have regressed from nature's advance echelon of organic life. Humans will have dropped back to nature's rear ranks.

Other forms of life have "achieved this victory." There is no question that it can happen. The question is: Can those who are pushing the human species toward regression be stopped? That is what concerns all who look to nature and nature's god as the only reliable guide from which to take our direction.

If we have eyes to see, we see the petty distinctions between the various dogmas used to oppose individual sovereignty as wholly unimportant. The Old Testament dogma that was condemned by Jesus — the dogma proclaiming a magician-like creator whose directions had to be interpreted by priests — serves exactly the same purpose as the equally ridiculous dogma that matter is prior to creative intelligence, and that *matter* is the creator of *human* creative intelligence. These are tweedle-dee tweedle-dum dogmas that can be used by a clique of self styled "authorities" to manipulate unperceiving mobs for the purpose of controlling dissenting individuals.

Among what is usually called "primitive" peoples, "authority" is based on the claim that the leaders and priests have a special "super"-natural knowledge. The "one and only true god" that purportedly imparts this "super"-natural knowledge to special individuals is continually replaced with another "one and only true god." As people become more sophisticated, serpent-makers invent new sources for "authoritative" dogmas. The current "one and only true god" of the pseudo-scientists, who are the new bred of serpent-makers, is Matter.

The dogma of the pseudo-scientists, which is based on even less perception than that of the primitives, is that Matter created intelligence "by accident." No perceptive scientist would leap over the mountains of unexamined evidence and present such a totally unsupported dogma as "scientific fact." However, perceptive scientists, who gave us much solid knowledge of reality, are now being pushed aside. Pseudo-scientists, committed to serpent-making, already control the tax-supported academic system and the government-licensed media.

The "scientific facts" of the pseudo-scientists, the priests of Popular Materialism, are as completely unsupported as the "supernatural" dogmas they are replacing. And the requirement that one show acceptance of these dogmas, and commit years to their study, before being admitted to the ruling "scientific" clique, is no different from commitment to years as a neophyte in any other priestly hierarchy. The requirement makes it difficult to throw away the years of study by opposing the dominant dogma.

The facts accepted by those who gained a good name for science are these: (1) Reality cannot be reduced to words nor to mathematical formulas. (2) Neither one human, nor all the combined humans in the world, can perceive a sufficient portion of total reality to offer an "authoritative" interpretation in words or mathematics for the direction of others. (3) Nature — the total reality — is the only reliable guide. (4) There is some sort of system of natural selection that has been in operation for an estimated 300,000 times as long as the known history of humans.

Alongside the above, we must measure the known activities of the human species. Human culture of corn, beans, fruit trees, milk cows, et cetera, has overruled natural selection in breeding for variations that provide humans with food. The serpent-culture, which breeds out individual integrity and perpetuates the unperceptive who can be dogma-controlled as groups, has overruled natural selection of humans. This serpent-directed human-culture-of-humans probably predates food cultures; it probably began when humans were in the hunting or food-gathering stage. This human-culture-of-humans is not ''the way things are'' *in nature.* Its opposing direction should be carefully examined.

The scant history of the Northern Europeans that has not been destroyed by serpent-makers indicates that these segregated peoples recognized the opposition of the serpent culture to natural selection. They consciously created a different culture — one that would help compensate for the harm already done to the human species. They created a human-culture-of-humans that would accelerate natural selection by *restraining* group domination of individuals. This effort to reverse the anti-nature direction of the primitive serpent-culture has been drastically mutilated. It is in danger of being totally destroyed.

Let us expand the question of: What can be done? Expanded it becomes: Why has the serpent way of life overruled individual sovereignty? What will be the end result if it is continued? If we want to avoid that result what can be done?

John Harland has given answers to these questions in his brief history called *Word Controlled Humans.* In this paper, I am amplifying some points he made from a different perspective.

The significant weakness of the Northern Europeans was that their total segregation from serpent ways for untold centuries cost them their immunity to ''serpent poison.''

Jesus was born in the middle of serpent cultures and had intimate experience of the most underhanded serpent ever known. He learned from that experience. He told his disciples that, if they understood what he had tried to teach them, they could handle serpents and not be harmed.

We, who have a multitude of serpent-makers in our midst, have now undergone enough contact so that our immunity should have been restored. It has not. That is unfortunate. We now face what the serpent-makers present to us as two radically different factions fighting each other. They encourage us to take sides. Some of us do not look closely enough to see that it is not factions; it is one serpent with two heads. Some of us have become immune to Judaeo-"Christianity." Few are immune to the new serpent poison of pseudo-scientific dogma.

I recognize that it is going to be very difficult in this paper to pick a course through the obstacles set up by serpent-trained pseudo-scientists. But it is necessary to run that course in order to point out the difference in direction between the way of life compatible with individual sovereignty and the way of life promoted by the pseudo-scientists.

One need is to look at organic realities and examine evidence that serpent-trained pseudo-scientists insist does not need a new examination. They do not want anyone to lift the veil of dogma they have imposed on the evidence.

Another need is to look at social dogmas that the serpent-trained sociologists, psychologists, and politicians, as well as the anti-Christ "Christian" ministers, and the Jew-dominated media insist should not be questioned.

We must walk through the snake pit, past the serpent-haired bright Medusa. Those who have no immunity to serpent poison may not make it through.

The organic realities are those relating to sex. The social dogmas are those relating to group-regulated marriage and the suppression of maleness and femaleness.

The highly important questions, which have long been veiled by dogma, are these: Why did organic life become male and female? How does a difference between male and female fit into the whole of nature? How *should* this

difference between male and female be fitted into a human-controlled culture of humans? These questions involve us in both biological and "behavioral" fields. Dogmas designed to distort perception are plentiful in both places. Sex is the most formidable organic reality that opposes the direction of serpent-makers.

The question of why there is male and female organic life has always been sluffed off by serpent "educated" pseudo-scientists. They have always given it some such perfunctory dismissal as "sex exists because it happened accidentally and had survival value; the value that enabled it to survive was the fact that it made for more rapid variation and faster evolution." The perfunctory answer has not yet been modified to accommodate recent studies of fossil structures, which purportedly show that sexual and asexual variations occurred on time schedules of equal duration. But, if the new evidence is accepted, a new perfunctory answer will doubtless be forthcoming. Where there is a will to adhere to a position that serves the serpent-maker's purpose, a way will be found.

I view sex as being the most glaring evidence that creative intelligence was a functioning part of nature long before humans arrogated to themselves the name of Home sapiens.

Those who want to *create* serpents, want an *exclusive* field for the exercise of creative intelligence. Such "supernatural" advocates as Moses claim to get their dogmas from voices unheard by others. The pseudo-scientists make use of the *reaction* to this. They say that they have no creative intelligence; they say that the words coming out of their mouths are the actual words of their new god Matter; they claim to be computer-like spokesmen translating into words — with mechanical faithfulness — what goes into their mechanical senses.

While proclaiming that there is no such thing as creative intelligence in the natural universe, they make a great effort to oppose nature. They make a great effort to *create* a priestly hierarchy of pseudo-scientists that will supply continuing dogmas useful to the new priests. It is the old serpent with a new face; it is the false Yahweh replaced by the equally false god, Matter, whose words are called "statistical probability." The priestly pseudo-scientists *create* the statistical probability by the statistics they *choose* to observe.

Bringing the meaning of organic life and sex into full consciousness, as a basis for cooperative action between individuals, means going outside *two* serpent thought patterns: The Judaeo-"Christian" dogma that there is a non-natural god that rejects his own creation and seeks "victory over nature." And, the pseudo-scientific dogma that human creative intelligence is an accidentaly manufactured computer. It means postulating that: (1) Organic life is not a plaything created by a magician-like god, and (2) organic life is not an accidental arrangement of matter.

The conceptual basis for individual sovereignty, whether individual sovereignty be called "the way of the early Northern Europeans" or "the teachings of Jesus," is a postulate that creative intelligence is the aboriginal first cause — the "Father" of *all* organic life. This suggests that, after we have discarded the dogma of a magician-like creator, we examine organic life without ruling out *before the evidence is examined* the possibility that organic life is a creative venture of an intelligence prior to Homo sapiens. This means examining a postulate that the same creative intelligence which exists within ourselves is the *progenitor* of organic life, that the aboriginal creative intelligence did not stand outside organic life — that creative intelligence *became* organic life. It means postulating that *all* organic life, which gives evidence of being creatively intelligent, *is* creatively intelligent. It means postulating that the speck of green scum floating in the ooze has the purpose and direction of a god adventuring into a new form of creation. It means postulating that the cells, which make up an asexual animal, are intelligent and have creatively formed a multicelled organism — a "civilization" of cells. It means postulating that organic life continues unchanged for long periods of time and then comes up with a sudden, completely different mutation because the "civilization of cells" is a "civilization" of intelligent, cooperative entities, who have *created* a variation for the new organic structure.

If we begin with the above postulate *that fit the observed realities* then, by examining the creative intelligence within ourselves and observing the workings of contemporary creative intelligence objectively, can we go on to postulate a purpose that would cause the asexual to create the sexual mutation?

Asexual reproduction is entirely adequate for reproductive purposes. If reproduction were the *purpose* of sex, then there would be no impulse by a creative intelligence, and certainly not by blind force channeled by accident, for the cells to create a male and female. The complication would accomplish nothing.

Everyone readily understands why single cells would create a civilization of cells. If humans were disembodied eggheads, or cells, a multicelled asexual animal would be the realization of the serpent-maker's objective. Perhaps the existant human society has already regressed so far that it is now functioning on the level of a cell civilization — or "aspiring" to do so.

The evidence indicates that the cells of a multicelled organism have fully accomplished everything that people, who respond to serpent-dogma, have tried to do in the twentieth century. The cells are radically different but "equal under the law." Politicians have nothing to oppose. Women's lib has nothing to oppose. Homosexuals have nothing to oppose. There is no male and female. The cells are unsexed "citizens."

Unless another objective is *inherent* within it, such a "civilization" — made up either of cells or of dogma-controlled humans — will have but one objective: That objective is to grow, absorb all other organic life, rediscover the past practice which the green scum cells used in making nourishment from inorganic material and then populate the entire universe.

If the inherited intelligence of the cells had been mutilated by forced conformity to serpent-dogma, they might have proclaimed to each other: "There is no god. There was no creative intelligence before we came along. But we, who have created this great civilization, could do so because we have accidentally developed creative intelligence. We will create a god; we will achieve victory over nature."

It is easy to postulate that the cells that thought like that may not have been bred out of existence. However they did not create sex. Those that did create sex were those that bred true to their heritage of creative intelligence. They did not think of an objective god. They thought: "I am in the Father and the Father is in me." They had reverence for all nature, as the cherished past of their own creative intelligence. Also, they recognized that oneness, as an objective, was not furthering creation; it was regression to what had been before organic life. They sought a further creative adventure *in the self-chosen direction of limiting omnipotence.* They sought a direction *that did not have total re-absorption of the universe and return to oneness* as its objective.

Further creation by the cells making up the multi-celled asexual organism had two conflicting impulses: One was: Create by selecting other organisms for preservation; then gather the selected into a universe of the chosen. The other was: Create by selective destruction of what clutters up and opposes the new creation.

The solution provided by the mutation creating sex was: Separate the two opposing impulses that are now under one control. Make two separate individuals. Make one direction dominant in each. Make further propagation conditioned on an individual to individual reuniting of the different creative impulses. This solution became a reality. A female and male were created by the "civilization" of cells.

Among the *many* advantages resulting from the creation of sex, two are of vital concern in the conflict between individual sovereignty and the serpent way of life: (1) Sex injects a new selective factor into survival. It breeds for perception. It imposes on the creative impulse within each individual the need to *observe* an *utterly different* creative impulse in one of the opposite sex. This stimulates a subjective-objective pattern of perception. The previous asexual view that all organic life other than oneself was mere substance to be used or discarded is balanced by an objective interest in other selfs. The opportunity and encouragement for individuals to respond to this subjective-

Michigan Christian College Library
Rochester, Michigan

objective balance is made a condition of species survival. (2) Sex places a road block across the impulse to return to oneness. By requiring that each individual intimately know — by objective perception, not by absorption and digestion — at least one organism utterly different from oneself, sex sets a creative direction opposite from the impulse to return to oneness.

Let us go back to our postulate that creative intelligence is not making playthings — that the creative intelligence commits its very being to its creations. In a female or a male — as incomplete beings — courage, daring, and love are now required to say "I am, I perceive, and I will." Life is thereby enriched, made more intense. But a problem has developed. By the time sex has become fully established, full memory that omnipotence and oneness *were abdicated to achieve still greater creation* is becoming dim. The self thus isolated by the perceived incompleteness of its sexual being has the danger of feeling frightened and insecure. The unperceptive — in whom the knowledge that "I am in the Father, and the Father is in me" has dimmed to virtual non-existence — wants to inflate its "ego." It wants to disregard the discipline of sex and revert to omnipotence.

Sex is the road block against the return to oneness.

Development and expression of the herd instinct is a concession some wild animals make to that return-to-oneness impulse. That concession can be pushed too far. Serpent makers use dogma to push it.

All serpent-makers have a strong, conscious or subconscious *opposition* to sex — not to the sexual act, as an ego-gratifying, sensual-pleasure to be indulged as an idiot slobbers over food — but opposition to sex, itself, as something pressing for perceptive attention.

All serpent-making contains either a conscious or subconscious attempt to destroy sex — to the extent that it opposes serpent-making. Unfortunately, most serpent-makers do not have enough perception to recognize that there *can be no half way measures.*

Sex, as a road block against the impulse to return to oneness, *has been completely destroyed* by the "social" insects — more correctly: the *regressive* insects — ants, some species of bees, and termites.

Instead of word dogmas, odors — principally the sex odor of the "queen" — more correctly: *the one female still capable of reproduction* — are used to bind the physically separate individuals into one organism. This organism of multicelled organisms is, in most respects, little different from a simpler "cell civilization" of asexual cells. The obvious difference is that it is an objectively observable civilization of physically discrete individuals.

The significant point is that the physically discrete individuals were once sexual beings. They have abandoned their past development and resumed the role of cells; they have become unsexed "citizens" of the "dogma" controlled group. Misused sex odors are the "dogma" for "victory over nature."

In these regressive ("social") insects can be seen the end result of our present human civilization's current direction. The similarities are glaring. Some ants, like present day humans, continually wage war.

Every nation in the world is now moving in the direction of the regressive insects. The tweedle-dee versus tweedle-dum choices being offered in human civilizations can be seen objectively in ant, bee, and termite civilizations.

Let us look at the kind of fully accomplished "civilization" that would result if the current serpent-makers in the United States were to become successful in subjecting everyone to their proposed group-organism-state. The East African termites appear to be the closest parallel.* These termites are not an ant species; they are related to the cockroaches; they are vegetarians. The East African termite "civilization" is not an aggressive "nation," as are some of the ant "civilizations." It fights only defensive wars. The termite soldiers are all unsexed females. The workers are all unsexed males. Reproduction is accomplished by having one female modified to become an egg producing factory. This modified female no longer appears to be of the same species

*See *Dwellers in the Dark — Termites,* article and photographs by Glenn D. Prestwich, Ph.D., NATIONAL GEOGRAPHIC, April 1978.

as the other modified females. She — or more correctly *it* — *is* a reproduction factory. *It* is the sort of reproduction factory described in Huxley's book, ironically titled *Brave New World. It* has increased in size to a helpless monstrosity, hundreds of times the size of ordinary termite individuals. Workers manipulate it; they run the factory. The male, whose act of mating enables the factory to produce eggs, remains original size. The factory will produce about two hundred million new "citizens" — *parts* of the whole, *things* neither sexual nor asexual.

This regressive "civilization" which, in its effort to return to oneness, has mutilated and overrun the road block of sex — has existed for longer than the human species, even longer than the dinosaur. However, the green scum floating in the swamp has existed still longer.

Suppose we postulate that survival is not life's only purpose. Suppose we postulate that acquiring an ever greater knowledge of such things as green scum, the composition of feces, and methods for preserving and propagating the congenitally incompetent, and the way to "free individuals from the burden of reproduction" and give them more "constructive pursuits" is a perverted use of the elaborate human brain. Suppose we postulate that the creative intelligence within Homo sapiens is our natural heritage, that nature is our guide, and take it from there. If we do that, no further obstacle to unlimited creation exists *except the serpent-makers.*

The serpent-makers want to distract from perception of sex, because it is a road block across their regressive direction. The methods they use to oppose sex vary. The Judaeo-"Christian" serpent-makers originally wanted to make sex a taboo subject for conversation. The pseudo-scientist serpent-makers now want to class sex as merely "one of the many forms of reproduction." They want to say it is worthy of no special attention, and dismiss it. The serpent-makers in control of TV, movies, and the media want to confuse sexual perception by throwing in homosexuality and other forms of perversion as acceptable variations of the sex act, which they present as nothing more than a sensual pleasure.

All methods serve the same purpose. All seek to manipulate sex in some way that will remove the road block to the regressive direction of serpent-making.

The Northern Europeans had seen what the serpent-makers were doing. They committed themselves to stomping on the serpent and slaying the dragon. They also developed a way of life that respected sex so highly that their *way of life* was a consciously constructed *road block* against *serpent-making.*

I want to accent the *differences in direction* between the serpent-culture and the culture of individual sovereignty — when both are seen as human-cultures-of-humans. The culture of the early Northern Europeans and the culture of the Jews provide the best available comparison of the two directions.

CHAPTER 6

The sexual attraction, the inborn impulse for a male and female to approach, examine, and come to know each other, is the key that opens the door to the balanced, subjective-objective perception of nature's god. The perceived time-movement of creative intelligence from omnipotence-and-oneness to the limited-power-and-diversity of organic life is part of the panorama on which the door opens. Either as a consciously imagined projection, or a re-awakened subconscious memory, the whole is known, and the staggering magnitude of the adventure experienced. Love of a mate, whose creative impulses are counter to, but at the same time in harmony with one's own, broadens perception to embrace the whole panorama of vital continuity. Inborn knowledge becomes conscious knowledge. Oneness and otherness is consciously recognized as the background melody of being that allows for unlimited variations on the theme long ago sounded.

After children are born, the parents are stimulated to examine their relationship to the whole universe even more than before. They feed the children, give them shelter and clothing. Being dependent, the children do what they are told. This feeds parental egotism. Parents sometimes have a short-sighted impulse to push the children into doing what *they* want done, so as to honor themselves. Sometimes, there is even an impulse for the parents to make the children into extensions of themselves. However, if they have been sensitive to the significance of maleness and femaleness, they will have learned one of the lessons sex has to teach: They will have perceived that the pattern of the vital continuity is abdication of power, and they will want to add their beings to that pattern. They will encourage their children to see with their own eyes, hear with their own ears, focus on the creative intelligence born within them, and relish the adventure of being.

Among humans, there is a constant danger that elaborate language will deflect sex-taught perception.

The individual is even more easily controlled by the social group than children by parents. Children soon become as physically powerful as their parents. They can assert themselves. They can fight against their parents and have a fair chance of winning. Group power is too great for an individual to fight. If the group sets a blueprint and the individual does not want to follow it, overwhelming group force can become group tyranny.

As soon as it was discovered that words could be used to form dogma-controlled groups, those who did not learn what sex had to teach formed groups to dominate dissenting individuals. The dragon was created by the unscrupulous. Within the dragon society — under a facade of giving medicine-man-aid to the sick, taking over the tedious aspects of educating the children, or "explaining" a "religion" based on invention of non-natural "gods" — the surreptitious serpent was created by those who were more unscrupulous than the dragon makers. The dragon destroyed the whole being. The serpent destroyed only the creative intelligence within; it preserved the body and made of it a dogma-controlled zombi that could be used to make other zombis.

As first known to recorded history, the Northern Europeans had obviously found dragon and serpent societies repulsive. They had rejected them. We know this from three sources: (1) The temperament bred into the people themselves. (2) The fragments remaining of their ballads that recited admired behavior. (3) The writings of Julius Caesar and Tacitus. All three clearly show that they had developed a unique society which successfully restrained group dominance of individuals. Slay the dragon and crush the serpent was their policy in dealing with the rejected societies.

In lieu of a wall, they had created a no-man's land around themselves. Segregation was essential. The strength of their defense against intrusion was impressive. But the methods devised for preventing the unscrupulous from forming dogma controlled groups, and destroying dissenting individuals *among themselves,* are what merit the most careful attention.

Killing in competition for survival was recognized as a natural condition of all organic life, so they saw nothing in nature to indicate that killing, itself, was immoral. However, they recognized that the dogma-controlled people of the dragon and serpent societies killed for *motives* that were immoral. They used gangs of the unperceptive, who could be controlled by dogma, to kill off the perceptive. That sort of killing was obviously opposed to nature's direction of breeding for the finest, and was, therefore, immoral. To devise a defense against anyone forming a dogma-controlled group in their midst, they had gone beyond a simple *return* to natural animal instincts and innate morality. They created a human-culture-of-humans. They accented nature's direction by a formalized yes-saying to nature's way. They conceived a way of life based on putting the perceptive social group's full power behind a demand for personal honor.

Personal honor was a *positive* concept regarding killing and mortal combat. Individual sovereignty was paramount. Nature's way had conscious defenders. Everyone was on guard against anyone trying to form a dogma-controlled group to enforce group will on dissenting individuals. No discussions ever took place without everyone being fully armed. Honor required everyone to meet a personal challenge, or forever after have the contempt of the whole society. An unscrupulous demagog could be challenged *as an individual — before* his dogma-controlled group began destroying opposition by the usual unscrupulous methods of serpent-makers.

The ultimate tribunal for all disagreements was physical combat, but honor required that it be one against one in a fair fight. The code of honor prevented surreptitious or surprise killings of individuals by other individuals, or by unscrupulous gangs. When two or more persons ganged up on one, the entire community rose against them, as they would against outside invaders. An individual without honor was simply shunned. A group without honor was declared an enemy and then destroyed.

Killing, other than one against one in a fair fight, could take place only against an openly declared enemy. All dogma-controlled groups, or dragons, were permanently declared enemies.

Perception of, and approval of, maleness and femaleness permeated the whole society. Formalized group support of any individual man who wanted to challenge another individual man to a fair fight was the whole group's yes-saying to maleness. The whole group recognized the innate prerogative of each individual to the essential role which destructiveness must play in an organic world. The people fully recognized that selective breeding is based on two factors — birth and death — *and there are no others.*

In the serpent-dragon societies, against which the people were defending themselves, the *group* dealt death to those who opposed *unscrupulous leaders;* and the *group* encouraged birth among those who were *unperceptive and easily controlled by dogma.* The defense against this practice was to give group sanction to every man's prerogative to deal death *as an individual decision,* provided it was a fair fight. Every woman had the same *unqualified individual* prerogative in choosing the man by whom she would bear children.

Observers were impressed that these people had an almost unbelievably great faithfulness in mating. Although the Mediterranean observers used the word "marriage" when referring to the relationship, there was no "giving in marriage" that required group or priestly determination of what was "holy" and what "adulterous." A woman's formal acceptance of a man as her mate was what observers designated by their accustomed term "marriage." However, the Northern European woman's acceptance was entirely her own publicly announced choice; there was no parental "giving" and priestly "sanctifying." This *highly important* distinction between (1) a woman's *absolute* control over her choice of a mate, and (2) the injection of group or priestly voices into the mating — was apparently not noted by outside observers. However, outside observers were impressed, and did note, that a Northern European woman was looked upon, and her words heeded, as if she were a goddess.

Children were discouraged from mutilating their perception of sex by having sexual relations before fully adult. Caesar said that it was a point of pride among the males to have no sexual relations before they were at least twenty years old.

The nearest approach to what Caesar called a "king" was very little more than public acclaim given to one who evidenced the best in heritage and behavior. This was not a *position* having a king's "authority" as Caesar thought of kings.

One individual's obedience to the will of another was always based upon personal agreement. An army was formed when an objective was announced in open assembly. Those who wanted to follow a leader in accomplishing the stated objective made a personal agreement to take their tactical directions from him. This meant instant and absolute obedience. Having made such an agreement, they considered it disgraceful to leave a field of battle without accomplishing the stated objective if their leader had been killed and had not given an order to retreat. Personal honor of leader or followers was all that earned respect. There was no concept that anyone could have honor or prestige simply by having a "position."

Honesty and personal integrity were the traits that most distinguished the Northern Europeans in the eyes of others. The unscrupulous made use of these unusual traits to destroy them. The Romans enticed them into becoming the fully trusted first line of military power surrounding the Roman emperor, and, as such, they fought their own people. Also, their unfamiliarity with stealth and lies made them vulnerable to the anti-Christ "Christian" manipulators. Even in Shakespeare's day they had not yet been fully convinced that one "may smile, and smile, and be a villain still."

The concept of "ownership" was fully recognized and

fully rejected. One of the duties given to the "king," who was chosen for his demonstrated good judgment along with all the other qualities that the people admired, was to re-assign areas each year, so that the people would not fall into the trap of having pride in possessions. Their only inviolate possessions were weapons. These were not thought of as "owned." Sometimes they were considered as much attached to oneself as one's skin. At other times they were viewed as one's parents or one's children were viewed. Swords were given names just as parents and children had names. They were not "owned"; they were trusted companions.

The infiltrators imposed the muddy concept of "ownership" in the same unscrupulous manner that the concept of marriage is, even now, imposed by a commandment "Thou shalt not commit adultery." This commandment leads to the unexamined *implication* that group control in a woman's choice of a mate is an essential factor of morality. The priests played the same game in imposing the concept of "ownership" on the Northern Europeans. They said that taking anything that another had once used was "stealing," taking by stealth. Stealth, along with lies, was the most contemptible of all actions. Because no one wanted to be accused of "stealing," the concept that the group had a moral prerogative to assign "ownership" was slowly accepted.

In summary, the Northern European culture bred for personal integrity, honesty, and individual perception.

Biblical Jewish history gives an example of breeding in the opposite direction. It is a human-culture-of-humans overruling natural selection so as to breed a controllable group. The well known Biblical story shows how this works.

Moses led the Jews out of Egypt. While planning the final act of sabotage that he knew would result in the Pharaoh driving them out, Moses told all the people to "borrow" as much gold and silver jewelry from the Egyptians as they could. Apparently they made quite a haul. The Bible says that they "wasted" the Egyptians. After they had been driven out, Moses went up on a mountain to figure out his next move.

While he was gone, his brother Aaron had the idea of forging the people into a controllable group by making them put all the gold and silver they had "borrowed" together and melting it into one chunk. This was done; they melted the jewelry and made it into a golden calf. Aaron, of course, could reason that: As their wealth, it would become a single group possession; and, as a totem, it would represent the group god. It was the customary move in the direction of groupism.

However, when Moses came down from the mountain, he was so contemptuous of the routine effort that he had the whole statue ground up, mixed with water and made the people drink it. Maybe he felt the need for a dramatic effort to retake control of the people from Aaron. But Moses obviously had given more thought to serpent-making than his brother. He recognized that a serpent-maker's prime tool is dogma. Dogma was identified with his own totem. He presented the people with ten commandments that he said were the actual words written on stone by their god.

These commandments were typical of the dogmatic statements that became the basis for all primitive cultures of groupism. They set up the pattern for extending the control over children, begun by their parents before sexual development, into group control that represses sexual differences and gives the group substantial control over maleness and femaleness in adults. The commandments, purportedly coming from an invisible god, told adults to follow the dogmas of their parents; they spelled out laws that would be used to keep adults acting as if they were still children.

The two facets of sex, that, after puberty, became impulses distinguishing adults from children, are creation by selective destruction and creation by what is selected to preserve and cherish.

Among the Jews, the male was deprived of all individual choice in perceptively exercising the impulse toward selective destruction. *Individuals* were given an unequivocal dogma: "Thou shalt not kill." The female had the restriction of parental and group pressure placed on her sexual perception, and her choice of a mate. The woman would be "given" in marriage; the priest, speaking for group "authority," would validate the marriage as "holy."

The group control was made absolute by the primitive concept that the group would tell each individual what that individual "owned." As usual, the commandments did not honestly state what was being done. The process by which "ownership" came to exist was ignored. The commandments merely said that no one should take, or covet, what was "owned" by someone else.

Any perceptive person, looking at those commandments, would see that "position" and accumulated "possessions" would become the things valued highest in the Jewish way of life. It would be clear that the Jewish culture would both breed and train for constant scheming in order to "own" things and gain a "position" that would "authorize" one to manipulate group control. There were some who had enough perception to object to the commandments.

Then came the first day of the cultural selection, which showed how this total package of dogmatic-group-control worked. The dogma said to the individual: "Thou shalt not kill." It did not honestly say "Thou shalt not kill *except* as one of the power-group forcing the dogma "Thou shalt not kill" on *others*. But that was the way it worked:

Moses said, "Who is on the LORD's side? ... And all the sons of Levi gathered themselves together unto him. And he said unto them, Thus saith the LORD God of Israel, Put every man his sword by his side and go in and out from gate to gate throughout the camp, and slay every man his brother, and every man his companion, and every man his neighbor. And the children of Levi did according to the word of Moses, and there fell of the people that day about three thousand men." Exodus 32: 26-28.

The forked tongue way of the serpent should never be forgotten.

There are two directions in which the human species can breed. There are no others. All else is an attempt to make a confused mix of the two, which will give the advantage to those skilled in — and unscrupulous enough to prefer — underhanded actions. The two directions are diametrically opposite. They can be clearly stated.

One is the way of dogma-controlled groups, the way of the serpent, the way of the regressive insects.

The other is the way of individual sovereignty, the direction manifest by nature and nature's god.

Since most of the gains that had already been made against primitive dogma-control by the early Northern Europeans have now been lost, the "kingdom of heaven" is further away from realization than it was 2,000 years ago. Now the greatest hope rests upon the fact that there are still some descendants bred by that culture, who are uncomfortable in the non-natural culture now being forced upon us. We want to change direction.

Because people who are products of opposing cultures — that cannot be mixed — are now thrown together, the separation of those who want to go in each of the two opposing directions may be difficult.

But this much is certain: Nothing can be accomplished, and there can be no peace, until those committed to opposing directions are segregated.

CHAPTER 7

Giving attention to the methods of serpent-makers uses time and energy that all who are repulsed by serpent-making would prefer to use in ways that are more constructive. But, while there are serpents, it is necessary to pay enough attention to their ways so as to be able to handle them.

While taking over power from the Roman "authorities," the Roman-church-serpent used the tactic that the Nomadic Jewish Nation had already used for over a thousand years when preparing to "eat up other serpents." That tactic is pretense of helplessness and humility. The pope told the emperor, and all the priests told the local administrators: "*We* are a *religion.* Power is political. *You* have the *power.*"

Serpent-making is a slow, insidious process. But there came a time when the "political power" kneeled; thereafter the king reigned because a crown was placed on his head by a pope. If we look at realities, and are not tricked by words, we perceive that: Power based on dogma-control is held by the dogma-controller.

Dogmatic "authority" is the same regardless of whether it is called "religion" or "politics." The so-called Roman "religion" ate up the Roman "political" power. At the same time it also ate up the individual sovereignty of the Northern Europeans.

When individuals are sovereign, their *way of life* encompasses religion, politics, science, culture, education — everything as an integrated whole. Living things cannot be divided into pieces, and the pieces put into separate bins. Individual sovereignty cannot be factored.

When dealing with groups, the way of the serpent is to divide people against people. When dealing with individuals, its way is to divide each individual against oneself. The method used is most easily described by reference to the classic serpent. The Jewish Bible is filled with dogmatic contradictions. They confuse; they destroy the clear thinking and personal integrity of anyone who accepts them as significant. Then, an "authoritative" interpretation is offered, dogma dominates perception.

The Roman-church-serpent combined the anti-Christ works of Paul and the dogmas of the Nomadic Jewish Nation with the teachings of Jesus, which opposed the other two. The priests called the contradictory conglomerate "religion" and used it to destroy all dissent. By making expedient interpretations of what they called "god's word" they sent one individual after another to the stake or torture dungeons. Any defender of those singled out for persecution was also persecuted. A mob was set against the defenders simply by calling them "anti-Christian."

The practice would have utterly destroyed a lesser people than the Northern Europeans. They were highly vulnerable; they did not know how to handle serpents. However, individual integrity and perception had been selectively bred into them for countless thousands of years. It was not destroyed.

The first loud voice of protest against serpent practices was that of Martin Luther. He demanded that the people be allowed to read the Bible for themselves.

The Bible contained the twisted, but still decipherable, words of Jesus *denouncing* dogma and "authority." It was the only literature to which the people could still relate. They no longer had a *positive* literature telling how life should be lived. Individual integrity had been the bright shining value in the concept of honor running through their own ballads of love and courage. The old ballads, telling how life is lived by free people, had been called "sinful" and "barbaric." They had been forbidden. Those reciting them had been burned at the stake, or slowly tortured to death.

After a thousand years, the serpent culture had bred, not a whole generation of vipers, but a few native serpent makers. Some of these came to America. They had learned the trick of calling dogmatic control "religion." They pretended that the "real" *political* power was exercised from across the sea. The new serpent-makers called their dogmatic, life-and-death control over the people "religious authority."

Roger Williams led the people's fight against this. He carried the fight for freedom from dogma-control further than Luther had gone. Because of Luther's gains, people could now read how Jesus taught that no dogma, no law, and no prophets had "authority" over the holy spirit within each individual. Based on these teachings of Jesus, it was possible to point out that nothing could properly be called "religion" that opposed individual sovereignty.

Reading the Bible for themselves, the people could also see that the meaning of "church," as Jesus used the word, was radically different from what the priests had told them. "Church" as Jesus used the word was not a serpent. They could see that Jesus gave no dogmatic "authority" to any priest or pope. They could now read what Jesus really said when he had "established" a church. They could read that, in the cited conversation between Jesus and his disciples, Peter showed that he recognized "the son of man" and "the son of god" as meaning one and the same thing. He showed his recognition of the fact that people have the holy spirit within themselves because they have a god *heritage.* Peter's perception caused Jesus to realize that, at last, his teachings were being understood. Jesus dealt in realities and taught by the use of concrete examples. Using Peter as a concrete example of a perceptive individual, he said, "upon this rock I will build my church and the gates of hell shall not prevail against it." "Church" is the English translation of the Greek, "kyriakos," which means "dedication to the universal creative intelligence — the basic mover within all reality."

Roger Williams showed that nothing could properly be called "religion" except the direct relationship between the individual and the universal creative intelligence — as that universal creative intelligence could be perceived within each individual. He condemned any attempt to control another's *way of life* by dogmatic "authority" as being something utterly different from what could properly be called "religion." He said that people who wanted to consider "religion" as a group should congregate and choose anyone who evidenced perception as their leader or minister. They should not submit to direction of their lives by "authorities" set over them by a "religious" hierarchy.

A century after Roger Williams, Thomas Jefferson, writing the Declaration of Independence, re-stated that same basic principle of individual sovereignty — in broader context. He re-asserted the whole Northern European cultural heritage — the heritage of a people who had originally segregated themselves from all dogma-controlled people.

Jefferson's statement was much wider in concept than that made by Williams. Also, Jefferson was not speaking solely for himself. He was carefully voicing the re-awakened heritage of all the American colonists; they had selected him to be their mouthpiece. *Their joint declaration was addressed to the whole world.* To reinforce what all were saying, *individuals* pledged to other *individuals* their lives, their fortunes, and their sacred honor. Their commitment in words was backed by action that honored that commitment to the death.

Williams was stating the priority of the holy spirit within each individual. Because he was opposing those who called their dogma "religion" he could make reference to the words of Jesus — the only literature to which the people could still relate.

Jefferson, in setting forth the total *way of life* acceptable to the American colonists, had nothing but people's retained perception of basic reality on which to build. This made his job difficult; he did it well; he, himself, considered the Declaration of Independence as probably the greatest achievement of his life.

The Declaration of Independence makes it clear that, whatever other differences the American colonists might have had, they were agreed on one fact: Nature and nature's god had created them as sovereign individuals and no government was acceptable that did not recognize that self-evident sovereignty.

This commitment to individual sovereignty surrounds the Constitution of the United States. Anyone who tries to put any other interpretation upon anything within the Constitution must be regarded — and declared — an enemy of the American people.

Jesus was the first articulate Christian to break away from primitive Judaism and re-assert fidelity to nature and nature's god. Jesus's words are still being twisted. The twisting began with Paul, the anti-Christ, who called his anti-Christ distortion "Christianity."

As Jesus was the first articulate Christian, Jefferson was the first articulate American to break away from the same primitive dogma-control and re-assert fidelity to nature and nature's god. Thomas Jefferson's words are now being twisted by many anti-Americans who pretend to be "good-Americans."

The anti-Americans take the words "all men are created equal" out of context and use them in ways diametrically opposed to what the words say when left in context.

The whole sentence reads:

> **We hold these Truths to be self-evident, that all Men are created equal, that they are endowed by their Creator with certain unalienable Rights, that among these are Life, Liberty, and the Pursuit of Happiness — That to secure these Rights, Governments are instituted among Men, deriving their just Powers from the Consent of the Governed, that whenever any Form of Government becomes destructive of these Ends, it is the Right of the People to alter or to abolish it, and to institute a new Government, laying its Foundation on such Principles and organizing its Powers in such Form, as to them shall seem most likely to effect their Safety and Happiness.**

In context the "equality" phrase can have only one meaning: *All* are born sovereign individuals. It is a statement upon which to predicate the assertion that a government can have only such sovereignty over individuals as the individuals choose to give it. To give that "equality" statement any other meaning is either maliciousness or an evidence of abysmal stupidity.

During our present century the phrase "all men are created equal" has been pulled out of context and used in many ways that are destructive of its purpose. I cite two.

Perhaps the least damaging of these is the one designed to bring discredit on Jefferson as a person. By itself, the statement "all men are created equal" is, of course, not true. His enemies quote it out of context, and then claim that Jefferson stated an obvious untruth in an attempt to make the Declaration appeal to poor, struggling people, when he was a wealthy landowner.

The more damaging twist ignores the fact that "all men are created equal," when taken out of context, is an untruth. The serpent-makers want to use the *untruth,* itself, as dogma. They claim that, because the words are in the Declaration of Independence, the United States Government is committed to *making* all men equal. Such an objective would mean that the United States was committed to set itself up against nature and nature's god. That is exactly what the serpent-makers *want.* The age-old objective of serpent-makers is "victory over nature" — and the victory of their non-natural gods over nature's god.

These misinterpretations are not made out of *purposeless* stupidity. They are made because they push a little further in the direction the serpent-makers are trying to go. Out of context the statement "all men are created equal" fits in with their direction. That direction is: Use the unperceptive group, that can be controlled by dogma, to destroy the perceptive. *Mobs* are their tools; they view individuals as nothing but mob-pieces. And if the integrity-destroyed humans are too incompetent to be used as their tools, they can still be used as animated counter chips. In an election they *are* equal — equal counters in the contest for power.

Seeing the words of Jesus and Jefferson twisted backwards is maddeningly offensive. But arguing over the meaning of the words, themselves, is playing into the hands of those who want *words* to be revered. When *words* are revered, they can be used to distort perception. Building up reverence for words is the first step toward building up reverence for dogma. The *way of life* is the whole picture that needs to be kept in focus.

In the Declaration of Independence, Jefferson recited specific offenses of the King that immediately concerned the colonists. Before doing so, he brought into focus the long range problem. The colonists were trying to reclaim the mutilated values of the early Northern Europeans. These values he restated.

He stated that segregation of one people from others — who do not acknowledge that governments are created by men — is the way clearly shown by nature and nature's god. The reference "god" is to the god of Jesus and the god of the Northern Europeans — nature's god — not Jehovah, or Yahweh, the monstrous *non-natural* god of the Jews. The re-assertion of that *nature-oriented way of life*, which had bred the Northern Europeans as different from other peoples, is the solid foundation upon which the United States is built.

These initial statements in the Declaration of Independence, which focus on a way of life, *are positive assertions* of things that are self-evident to all who have eyes to see.

Kings "by the grace of god," and those having fidelity to such kings are not specifically mentioned, but they are tacitly excluded from the new government being formed.

By the same clear positiveness, all citizens of the Nomadic Jewish Nation, who do not *entirely* renounce *and cease participation in that citizenship* are tacitly excluded as participants in the segregated people's new nation. Mortal enmity is inherent in the opposing ideologies of the two nations. The new nation is built on individual sovereignty. The Nomadic Jewish Nation is built upon the dogma that the Jews have a government purportedly instituted by their god — the non-natural Yahweh. This dogma is unequivocally opposed to the premises underlying the government of the United States.

The *positively stated* concept on which the United States is built is that governments are instituted by men, dissolved by men, and re-established by men, in such form as seems most likely to effect their safety and happiness. Therefore no one can honestly (here "honestly" means: Not a fifth column infiltrator) become a United States citizen who still has some degree of fidelity to a ruler who purportedly rules "by the grace of god," or still has some degree of fidelity to a nation purportedly formed by a word-using god and governed by laws in words supposed to have come from such a god.

The Declaration of Independence is the basic assertion on which the United States was founded.

It must, therefore, have top priority in the present controversy regarding interpretation of the First Amendment to the Constitution which reads: "Congress shall make no law respecting an establishment of religion, or prohibiting the free exercise thereof."

At present, there is much opposition to a dogma regarding basic reality, which is being pressured on children attending public schools under a facade that it is "science." What is clearly being taught under the facade of "science" is serpent-making dogma. Much of the pseudo-science being taught *denies* the very existence of a creative intelligence and, therefore, is "prohibiting the free exercise" of religion.

Attempts are being made to set up a defense against this pseudo-science by reclassifying ideas that serpent-makers have long called "religion" and injecting them into the teaching program of public schools as "science."

Great changes are urgently needed in the whole school system. But words are the stuff of dogma and arguments about words play into the hands of the serpent-makers. Regardless of the words in which it is clothed, dogma that opposes the foundation on which the Constitution stands endangers the very existence of the United States. It is time we learned how to handle serpents.

Our ancestors were deluded into believing there might be some basis for a choice between the dogma-controlled "religious" Roman-church-serpent and the dogma-controlled "political" Roman dragon. Any "choice" could only result in the individual's subjection to a dogma-controlled group.

The words "religion" and "science" for what is taught in the schools is the same old tweedle-dee and tweedle-dum of the serpent makers. The intent of the First Amendment cannot be furthered by choosing between (1) dogma control by Jews using Judaeo-"Christians" as their tools, and (2) dogma control by Judaeo-Communists using brainwashed

atheists as their tools. The difference between dogma purportedly coming from a fictitious, non-natural god, Yahweh, and dogma coming from pseudo-scientists, who assert that there is no such thing as creative intelligence, is not worthy of consideration. The foundation on which this government is built demands that anything acceptable within the United States as "science" ***or*** **"religion" must be based on** ***nature*** **and** ***nature's god.***

That foundation was laid by those who pledged to each other their lives, their fortunes, and their sacred honor. The determination as to whether that foundation now remains or is now destroyed must be something more than an argument over mere words. Nothing is gained by examining the "authoritative" definition of "religion" and "science." Serpent-makers already control the media. The controlled media can shout down any non-serpent definition — and loudly proclaim which definition, idea, or opinion about anything is "authoritative."

The serpent controlled media has already twisted the words of the Constitution and come up with the constantly repeated mis-statement that: "The constitution of the United States insures freedom of religion."

Without helping the serpent-makers hone their weapon of words by going into a discussion of word-meanings, let us look at a couple of *examples* of "religious" group-control. After looking at such *examples,* we can look again at the misinterpretation of the First Amendment now being pressured upon the American people.

This story, from J. Cameron Grant's *Ethiopia,* has an additional interest (apparently not noted by the original observer) because it graphically demonstrates the, conscious or subconscious, antagonism to maleness and femaleness, which is always present in the "religions" of serpent-makers. This event, which purportedly was witnessed February 26, 1888, involves building a temple to a god. The words "temple" and "god" qualify it for the media's definition of "religion."

The day before the temple raising, the observer examined the site. Several large pilings that would form the basic framework for the temple had been cut. Holes had already been dug for the pilings. The holes impressed the observer as being unnecessarily big; they looked more like graves. However, their oversize made some sense to him because the heavy pilings would have to be raised by many hands and could not be dropped vertically into appropriate size holes.

The temple-raising day was one with tension in the air. Activity was all around. The people were not congregated in any one place.

At the temple site, the occasion was dramatized by much ceremony, chanting, and dancing in weird costumes. Then, from the village, with a new ceremony, with more dancing and weird costumes, several couples were brought to the site. Each couple consisted of one naked male and one naked female bound together. (The observer never determined how they had been selected.) With a chant, whose meaning was unclear, a bound couple was dropped into each of the several holes. When this had been done, a new dance followed.

Then all attention turned toward the village. Loud cries arose from those surrounding the temple site. The cries were a chant proclaiming readiness for the big event. Apparently something additional was to come from the village. The cries called for "the women."

At last they came, rigged out in ceremonial finery, a great procession, perhaps fifty women, each carrying a long heavy pole with a fuzzy decoration at the top and a metal shoe on the bottom end. With serpentine ramifications, and ritualistic dance steps, they surrounded all the holes. They poised their long poles. At the beginning climax of the ceremony, they jabbed the poles violently into the holes and chanted wildly as they pounded the couples into a bloody pulp. When the excitement was at its highest, the pilings were set on top of the bound couples while they still screamed. Then the piled dirt was thrown in and packed with great enthusiasm by all the group. The temple had its basic foundation.

If this happend in the United States would the media still hold to the interpretation that "the U.S. Constitution guarantees freedom of religious worship?"

Since that example might be dismissed as one observer's unconfirmed story, suppose we look at one that has full documentation: Moses came down from a mountain bringing stone tablets containing ten commandments — of which one was "Thou shalt not kill." Some followers of Moses were willing to believe that the commandments came from the god that Moses said had made them a chosen people. Others were not. According to the Jewish Bible, Moses told those who accepted his assertion that the commandments came from god: "Thus saith the LORD God of Israel, Put every man his sword by his side, and go in and out from gate to gate throughout the camp, and slay every man his brother, and every man his companion, and every man his neighbor. And the children of Levi did according to the word of Moses; and there fell of the people that day about three thousand men."

If this happened in the United States would the media still hold to the interpretation that the First Amendment guarantees the followers of Moses freedom to obey the words purportedly coming from their god?

There was no intent by those who wrote and ratified the First Amendment to license the building of "religious" temples by those who believed that each piling for the temple should be set on a bloody, pounded but still squirming, male and female bound together.

There was no intent by those who wrote and ratified the First Amendment to license free exercise of obedience to a god who purportedly said, "Kill every man his brother, and every man his companion, and every man his neighbor" if the brothers, companions and neighbors do not believe a people's government is created by Yahweh, and Yahweh makes the laws.

The Jewish serpent cannot be classed as a religion — within the meaning of the First Amendment. It is a nation with a concept of government diametrically opposed to that upon which the United States is founded. The Nomadic Jewish Nation was founded on the dogma that its government was not instituted by men. It was founded with the avowed purpose of living off the milk and honey produced by people of other nations. It was founded with no fixed location. It is now a permanently deployed fifth column, whose first "four columns" have no permanent geographical location, and, therefore, cannot be made to answer for actions of the fifth. The intent of the fifth column, as an integral part of the whole scattered nation, has to be assessed by looking at the nation's whole history. For three thousand years, it has been a nation of spies and saboteurs, waging undeclared war on all nations with fixed locations. Citizenship in the Nomadic Jewish Nation is prima facie evidence that the individual is an active spy and/or saboteur.

The Jewish Bible tells us what happens when these people, who purportedly take their battle orders from a fictitious god, decide it is time to act. A gory record of purportedly god-commanded treachery runs through the Jewish Bible and throughout all subsequent history.

In the United States, the media is now dominated by a fifth column of the Nomadic Jewish Nation. Its fifth columnists hold their media franchise in conspiracy with subversive serpent-makers elected — with media help — to law-making and law-enforcing positions in the United States Government. The substantial portion of the media that is controlled by the fifth columnists makes its basic appeal to the unperceptive. With the help of the subversive government law-makers and law-enforcers who cooperate in the controlled media's objectives, the proportion of unperceptive people in the United States is growing rapidly. Clearly the aim is to produce enough unperceiving, dogma-controlled voters to take over the United States Government by media-controlled majority vote.

Those who have been engaged in these fifth column activities, and those who have been giving aid and comfort to these undeclared enemies of the United States, are now clearly identifiable. We have restated, in the context of present conditions, the commitment to individual sovereignty on which the United States is founded. We have also restated the original, and still continuing, causes which impel us to a separation from others. Looking at the fifth column activities that are now taking place, a just respect for the opinions of mankind requires us to follow the re-stated basic Declaration with this specific statement of its application to current conditions: Those, who do not choose to abandon their fifth column activities, or their aid and comfort given to those engaged in such subversive activities, and commit themselves to the premises on which the United States is founded, should now leave all areas under United States jurisdiction. In spite of all efforts to cloud the basic issue involved, the reason for this statement remains clear.

The United States was founded on the concept of individual sovereignty as practiced by the early Northern Europeans and taught by Jesus. All memory of the early Northern European way of life has been replaced by the serpent-maker's false history that it was "barbaric." The words of Jesus have been twisted backwards. But the supreme statement made by his crucifixion remains:

One physical individual — a sovereign descendant of the universal creative intelligence, unconditioned by dogma — stood alone against the most clearly defined serpent known to history. Before all mankind, the crucifixion of Jesus proclaimed the mortal opposition that eternally exists in that relationship.

Erik Holden's comments on

THE SIX DISCIPLINES OF MAN'S BEING - Melvin Gorham

It is the good fortune of today's *real* Christians that Gorham has given us a story of creation that fits the early Northern European thought pattern. The pseudo-scientists, who have dominated the scene since the death of Sir Arthur Eddington in 1944 and Sir James Jeans in 1947, do not perceive reality; they *react* to *traditions*. Their reaction to the story of an incomprehensible magician-like creator making playthings borders on the psychotic. They react — but continue the primitive practice of looking at reality through the wrong end of the telescope. They simply set up Matter as another incomprehensible first cause, or god. To them, their new god, Matter, comes first, space is no more than the absence of matter, and time is reduced to a fourth dimension of space.

In *The Six Disciplines,* Gorham turns the telescope around so creation can be perceived from the viewpoint of one with a conscious heritage of creative intelligence. Observe the order of the subject matter listed in the table of contents:

The Problem.

The aboriginal "I am."

1. Awareness — the universe of time.
2. Objectivation of awarenesses — the universe of space.
3. Automation of the subconscious — matter.
4. Abdication of control — organic life.
5. Assurance of diversity — sex.
6. Approbation of diversity — man.

Some speculations regarding further disciplines.

Man's relation to government.

Gorham uses current language to describe what Jefferson called "Nature's God" and Jesus called "Father." This view of creation is like a breath of fresh air blowing away the odor of Judaeo-"Christianity's" decay.

Erik Holden, Founder of the
AMERICAN CHRISTIAN CHURCH

Erik Holden's comments on

WORD CONTROLLED HUMANS - John Harland

I highly recommend Harland's *Word Controlled Humans* as covering the significant facts of human history. Brief and crystal clear, it would be an admirable basic work before any other history is studied in the schools. The two major conflicting concepts of how life should be lived are described as cultural directions that came into conflict before that conflict reached a climax in the teachings and crucifixion of Jesus.

After the crucifixion, the path of the fork-tongued serpent culture is traced through Europe. The Holy Roman Church's use of a false Christianity to promote the serpent culture is sharply portrayed.

Then the American attempt to regain our cultural heritage of individual integrity is examined. The two hundred year long losing battle is covered from the perspective of religion, government, and money.

Expanding to the world wide scene, Harland looks at the errors made by the Germans under Hitler in trying to recover from the destructive effects of the serpent culture. He keeps his eye on what is significant rather than merely sensational.

This brief history puts the problems of the human species into a context where effective action to correct them can be seen as a present possibility.

The possibility for effective action within the United States — without bloody revolution — is precisely outlined in five detailed steps. There *is* a way out of the serpent culture — if we act NOW.

This book emphasizes the urgency for immediate action. It pinpoints problems. And it pinpoints what is *unquestionably* the only possible solution in the United States *aside from bloody revolution.*

Erik Holden, Founder of the
AMERICAN CHRISTIAN CHURCH.

SOVEREIGN PRESS

"Dedicated to Individual Sovereignty"

We proudly present

a representative sampling of our publications

74057 **THE SIX DISCIPLINES OF MAN'S BEING** bound with **MAN'S RELATION TO GOVERNMENT.** Melvin Gorham. A study of the life-direction pointed by evolutionary development and inherited memory, with special attention to the meaning of sex. A posited "ultimate frame of reference" for orienting individual life-direction and social development. Permanent quality, pocket-size paperback, 104 pages $1.50

After Nov. 15, 1982 the above pocket size edition will not be available. Revised edition will be:

82146 5¼ x 8¼ permanent quality paperback $5.00

81138 WORD CONTROLLED HUMANS, John Harland. This perceptive new author examines how the enslaving weapon of group force is directed and triggered by words. He shows how religious groups, mobs, lawful governments, and armies are all controlled by the same trigger. Harland holds nothing back as he points out those who have used this trigger, along with manipulated fear of force, to destroy the American dream. Finally he points out how words can be used to break the current enslavement of the American people. A book for all who would fight the growing power of the enemy in our midst.

81138 Hardcover $8.95

8112X 5 x 8 inches, permanent quality paperback $5.00

78081 **BRAVE NEW WORLD, A Different Projection.** John Harland. A multi-dimensional first book by a young rebel of the sixties generation looking at the establishment, at many well-known writings from Aristotle's *Politics* to Mark Vonnegut's *The Eden Express* and at various "alternate lifestyles" he and a runaway girl experienced. An unusual examination of current culture by a perceptive intelligence with a healthy animal perspective. Suitable for class room discussion. Permanent quality, pocket-size paperback, 151 pages $2.00

75065 **THE CURSE OF THE RING.** Melvin Gorham. A creative narrative-interpretation of Richard Wagner's *The Rhinegold*, transforming symbols of Pagan mythology into their present day counterparts in waking consciousness. This is the background work for Gorham's THE RING CYCLE. Permanent quality, pocket size paperback, 95 pages, illustrated $1.50

79111 THE RING CYCLE. Melvin Gorham. This tense adventure story, dealing with violence, political corruption, the meaning of sex, and marriage versus no marriage has appeal for the reader with or without a Wagnerian background. By magnifying a point of contrast, it brings the Garden-of-Eden and the older Babylonian story of two lovers in a garden to the reader's mind for new examination. Brunnhilde's *Gottingarten* is a place entirely separated from the serpent and her Pagan pantheism knows joy as the soul of creation. This clear, powerful portrayal of the spirit permeating the Northern Europeans of prehistory opens the door on a whole new world where intellect and emotions are in full agreement.

79111 Hardcover $8.95

79103 5¼ x 8¼ permanent quality paperback $5.00

7809X CENSORSHIP IN THE U.S. — I ACCUSE THE JEWS. Marguerite Pedersen. The editor of a current and continuing book publishing company points out that both Jewish and non-Jewish scholars have long recognized that the Jews are neither a race nor a religion; they are citizens of the Nomadic Jewish Nation, but this fact is suppressed by the media. Because it is not legally recognized by the U.S. Government, individual U.S. citizens have the full burden of resisting pressure from an entire alien nation which — obviously — no individual can do. Pedersen cites specific names, dates, and facts as examples of extremely widespread control of the U.S. media by an alien nation — with a U.S. Government agency effectively aiding the alien censorship. 5¼ x 8¼ paperback $3.00

70022 **PAGAN REALITY.** Melvin Gorham. A basic concept of the cause, reality, and purpose of the universe. This book examines all major religions of the world from the Pagan perspective. It sears more often than it praises, but does not leave a barren waste. Avoiding both the jargon of academic philosophy and the dogmas of "inspired" religious converts, it reaches a new plateau where being has meaning. 201 pages, 5 x 8, paperback $5.00

82146 AMERICAN CHRISTIAN BIBLE, Extracted by Thomas Jefferson. Together with **A New Declaration of Independence for Today's Americans,** Erik Holden. Covers: Christianity versus Judaeo-"Christianity," media manipulation of U.S. Government, controversy over First Amendment, pseudo-science versus creationism in schools, biological and sociological meaning of maleness and femaleness, the direction pointed by Nature and *Nature's* God, and much more.
82146 Permanent quality 5¼ x 8¼ inches, paperback $5.00

These can be ordered direct from publisher. Publisher pays postage (including foreign) when payment is included with order.
SOVEREIGN PRESS, 326 Harris Rd., Rochester, WA 98579 U.S.A.

Take 40 percent discount on 10 or more copies same title.

- - - - - - - - - - - - - - -

ORDER FORM

To: SOVEREIGN PRESS, 326 Harris Rd., Rochester, WA 98579

Please send me the following: I enclose $ ____________

Quantity	Title	Extension
	Sales tax (Washington residents)	
	Total	

Name ______________________________

Address ______________________________

______________________________ zip ________

MICHIGAN
CHRISTIAN
COLLEGE
LIBRARY
ROCHESTER, MICH.

Date Due